Sumitra *and* Anees

Sumitra *and* Anees

Tales and Recipes from a Khichdi Family

Seema Chishti

HarperCollins *Publishers* India

First published in India by HarperCollins *Publishers* 2022
4th Floor, Tower A, Building No. 10, Phase II, DLF Cyber City,
Gurugram, Haryana -122002
www.harpercollins.co.in

2 4 6 8 10 9 7 5 3 1

Illustrations: Ramnika Sehrawat

P-ISBN: 978-93-5489-588-3
E-ISBN: 978-93-5489-427-5

Typeset in 13/17 Perpetua at
Manipal Technologies Limited, Manipal

Printed and bound at
Nutech Print Services - India

This book is produced from independently certified FSC® paper to ensure
responsible forest management.

For Daanish, Sitaram, Akhila
and the
late Ashish Yechury

When
like a hailstone crystal
like a waxwork image
the flesh melts in pleasure
how can I tell you?
The waters of joy
broke the banks
and ran out of my eyes.
I touched and joined
my lord of the meeting rivers.
How can I talk to anyone
of that?

—Basava (translated by A.K. Ramanujan, from *Speaking of Shiva*)

❧

Haasil e husn au' ishq bas itna,
Aadmi aadmi ko pehchaane.

The essence of love is but,
That each human recognize the other.

—Firaq Gorakhpuri

Contents

Introduction

During the campaign for the Uttar Pradesh assembly polls in 2017, Prime Minister Narendra Modi loudly underlined the differences between the shamshan (crematorium) and qabristan (cemetery) in a bid to expose the supposed 'Muslim appeasement' of his principal rivals, the Samajwadi Party.[1] As much as it is said that words bandied about in the course of election campaigns in India must be forgiven and forgotten, this one cut deep.

So far so good, all faiths were said to lead us all to the same maker. Death, like birth, was a marker of mortality, thereby signifying something and unifying humans of all creeds. But now, by choosing to speak of places of eternal rest as labels for again reminding people how they differed from each other, the leader of our nation was signalling not unity but playing up our differences and sowing discord. In 2018, the National Investigation Agency was found investigating the reasons behind marital choices when it went after Hadiya, a twenty-four-year-old woman from

Kerala, for converting and marrying a Muslim. Hadiya's wasn't the only example of the government's prying into personal matters: new laws were introduced that now criminalized an adult decision for love, pitching it as a betrayal of faith and liable to attract long prison sentences as well.

So, we now live in a world where to marry outside your religion could attract not just a neighbour or the Khap's attention but lead to a full-blown crisis and confrontation with the law, forcing people to change names, jobs and cities and, in some cases, leading to loss of life or long years in jail. It has been a long and exhausting walk away from the idea that India is about the co-mingling of diversities.

The Indian subcontinent has been the crucible for centuries for diverse things to spawn and flower—quite the Amazon Forest of cultural diversity and coexistence. If this sounds like poetry, then the Constitution of the Indian Republic in 1950 rendered the idea in prose. It was so far ahead of its time. Well before even all Western democracies fully accepted the idea of universal adult franchise, the Constitution of India did. It refused to bow to the reigning prejudices and predilections of the time, of ethnicity, language and religion and empowered each of its children, people of all stripes and shades, with inalienable rights they could enjoy as Indians, equal in all respects.

A consequence of this incredible diversity, now codified in law, saw an India that belonged to everyone. Of course, not delivered perfectly to each of its children—there is plenty of unfinished business and inequity—but there was the right to free association, exercised in the most intimate of fields. To eat with, play with, work with and fall in love with people from diverse backgrounds was now legally possible. The modern Indian state said it stood for promoting fraternity. Fraternity was sought to be made a living proposition.

This is not nostalgia or making a case for India being a land of milk and honey. But the ground has shifted so much in the past eight years that it is important to mark the distance travelled from when equality and fraternity were written into the Constitution. Whether it is virulent hate speech exhorting people to kill or lynch, or ministers garlanding and attending the tricolour-wrapped funerals of people who led the lynching—there is very little being done to reassure minorities in our country that harmony matters and will be preserved. The 2019 Citizenship (Amendment) Act seeks to openly make India a place that welcomes only non-Muslims from three countries. Far from a state promoting fraternity, often the law and lawmakers in the Indian Republic appear to be in sync with some of the worst and most regressive societal impulses.

At a time of such virulent separation being attempted on our collective hearts and minds, some of us—born of marriages that defied the boundaries of caste or religion—feel exceptionally isolated. What was celebrated and thought of as exciting and quintessentially Indian is now portrayed as akin to a national security threat.

It was a young Syed Muslim man from the small town (now district) of Deoria in Eastern Uttar Pradesh who started a conversation with an older Kshatriya Hindu woman born in Arsikere, a small town in Karnataka, just as the republic had entered its teens. It was a conversation that led to a partnership of forty-two years, where the personal choices they made spawned a mini-India in the home they built together.

They met in 1964, the year India's first prime minister, Jawaharlal Nehru, died; and when their own time came Nehruvian India was on the wane.

Their story of fellowship will unfold in the following pages, along with a book of recipes that my mother laid out in order to preserve the several culinary traditions, from Karnataka and Uttar Pradesh, that she mastered during her lifetime. This book of dishes, of all kinds, routinely put down for a daughter she felt did not have the time to learn cooking, has acquired a different meaning now that people are being attacked for what they choose to eat, drink, read, and, of course, who they befriend or choose to spend their lives with.

Between them, Anees and Sumitra succeeded in demonstrating the essence of fellowship and cosmopolitanism. Growing up, nothing was a better primer to the finest things in life for me, whether an Amrita Sher-Gil print, a glass of Mysore rasam, a cane chair from Assam or a rare dictionary of the Andamanese language. My childhood moulded me in the context of multiple influences casually coexisting and stitched into our lives. A nodding familiarity with multiple languages and kinds of people was a given. Not just in the books, art, craft and sports discussed but in our lived lives. Long days were spent after school in social and political debates where I, an only child of working parents, would nod off on coffee house tables. Listening to music from the south, north and all other parts of the world addicted me to diversity and a respect and certain understanding of India, creating a sanctuary that allowed me to just be. I became confidently an *aadhi pixie, aadhi goblin*, as a school friend once described me. A 'mixed' home that eventually allowed the turbulence of who I was to blow around me and gave me the confidence to arrive at my own balance.

❧

Sumitra died on 3 March 2005.
Anees died on 10 October 2018.

It has been a rapid descent since, far away from the khichdi road into a loud cry calling for separation. And more separation. The anxieties that India thought it had pushed behind into the history books from 1947 have come right back to haunt it and shape its todays.

It is not as if all was hunky-dory in the seven decades since it threw off British rule and attained Independence. There was a lot that was cause for deep distress. Scholars have described it vividly over the decades. There was often violence that enabled the capture of democratic processes. This ensured that while democratic rules were formally obeyed, the grand goal of any democracy—of forging a sense of equality between each citizen—was subverted. But that was still in waves, in flashes of time and in the states. Nationally, there was a firm belief that Indian democracy had made it first past the post, ahead of Pakistan, Sri Lanka, Bangladesh and Myanmar, so that the danger of majoritarian control had passed. Just like businessmen and maharajas lost elections, so did overtly divisive candidates. There was a belief that Indian democracy had been able to provide the safety valves that ensured that the boat would not capsize, come what may.

India, it was hoped, would be the shining exception to the rule that South Asia was turning out to be. It was its own unique type, a marvel to have made it so long and so far.

There are many views on what made the republic suddenly vulnerable. Was it the long shadow of 1947 catching up, an inevitability of what should have been? Was it the explosion in the 1990s of economic deregulation, caste upheavals in north India and a renewed effort by the Hindu Right to push ahead with a drive to reclaim India as a land for just Hindus, the Hindu homeland?

After 2019, the re-election of the Bharatiya Janata Party (BJP) was interpreted now as the mandate to cut the cloth in the manner of what the Rashtriya Swayamsevak Sangh (RSS) blueprint had been in 1947. A series of symbols have been put in place to effect the switch without necessarily tampering with the Constitution in letter. The Central Vista is to be its most vivid sketch, but other than that, after the Ram Mandir has been secured at Ayodhya, with the Supreme Court judgment of 2019 paving the way for a Ram temple at the exact spot where the Babri Masjid stood,[2] primacy has been given to cows, followed by the 'protection' of Hindu women.

In the fast-paced technological as well as economic change that India was witness to since the 1980s, the BJP may, in hindsight, seem an inevitability. The 1980s and then the 1990s threw India into a churn that changed it fundamentally. It of course saw the rise of forces that challenged much of what was retrograde; the mobility, provided by the rising school enrolment rates, urbanization, mobile phones, technology and mass media shook shibboleths and threw open doors of interaction between castes, classes and religions. It afforded far many more opportunities of inter-mingling, 'mixing', leading often to breakdown of taboos to some extent and to more mixed marriages and certainly mixed romances. To those wedded to older ways of doing things or the certainty of old social hierarchies, the threat to the status-quo rang alarm bells. When a Dalit rode a horse through his village on his wedding day, or a Hindu and a Muslim couple decided to marry, it scared all those with a vested interest in the stability of the past. The rapid change ushered in the decades following the 1990s generated enough pushback from those who had a lot to lose. The backlash to the social upheaval of the '90s came in full force.

The number of rules infringing the ease with which those of different faiths/castes could get married under the Special Marriages Act, 1954, grew multifold. They now involve the police giving No-Objection Certificates and they even involve parental consent to what are patently adult decisions. The case of Hadiya, an adult woman studying medicine, marrying a Muslim man and its managing to waste several hundred hours of a Supreme Court bench would have embarrassed any another democratic country.[3] But in India, it was only a precursor of more unlawful 'laws' being introduced in states that now criminalize marriage between people of different faiths, much on the lines of what has happened in societies that have had deeply unhappy endings. The Nuremberg Laws in Germany or the Miscegenation Laws in the US explicitly forbade sexual relations and marital ties between Jews and non-Jews or between Blacks and Whites and had chilling consequences. In India, while it is yet to be seen how it all ends, the process of unravelling is certainly underway.

The point of preventing such marriages is not that these are plentiful. The National Health and Family Survey 2015-16 showed that such inter-faith marriages are only 2.5 per cent of total marriages; inter-caste marriages, by contrast, comprise 13 per cent, a significantly higher portion of the total. But what they do is demonstrate the possibility of breaking out of boundaries. Stereotypes get shattered with each marriage. It keeps people aware of what it is like on the other side of the ghetto, and in the long run prevents the demonization of minorities. This demonization is vital to keep stoking the cauldron of fury, which becomes that much harder to keep on the boil when love allows you to jump past those barriers. The opening up of the mind that follows and its possibilities and then the progeny of such marriages, all together take away from politics that thrives on separation and the creation of distances. These theories are easy to nurture and foment if there is zero contact between people of different faiths. For those who benefit from divides, conflict needs to be dusted up all the time, distances widened and new agendas of hatred pushed every day. That couples find each other, find love and happiness, discover a new shared identity, that romantic or conjugal relations nurture, means that they cross divides with a possibility of staying happily ever after, makes the Eternal Anger project much harder to keep going.

A law brought about in the autumn of 2020 via an ordinance in the middle of a global pandemic in India's largest state (Uttar Pradesh) is worth mentioning here. The Uttar Pradesh Prohibition of Unlawful Conversion of Religion Ordinance, 2020, was introduced by one of the most prominent poster boys of the BJP, Chief Minister Yogi Adityanath—the mahant of the Gorakhnath Math and a firm believer in his own version of Hindutva from his Hindu Yuva Vahini days. He and his politics are cognizant of the need to break the bonds of coexistence in its everydayness if a permanent majority for a Hindu

Republic must be developed and then kept going. This is a point eloquently developed by Sudha Pai in her book *Everyday Communalism*, where the conviviality or just sharing of non-hostile spaces—whether eating together, travelling, living or being buried/cremated side-by-side—is sought to be criminalized and the warp and weft of living together (and dying too) is torn apart. This ordinance which is now a law chimes with the deep-seated prejudices of all those who nurse the fear of having their identities diluted. Marriages in India have been the primary means of keeping caste alive and not just caste but religious and class differences too, with endogamy being the norm across society. It is trite to quote them, but the matrimonial columns in newspapers along caste and religious lines are a testimony to how strong social barriers are. In less fraught times, attempts have been made to minimize social divides but they are now amplified by majoritarian governments at the Centre and in the states. In fact, eight other states already have anti-conversion laws. Other BJP states would bring in similar laws, given that it has an obvious appeal to their base and more. Karnataka's version, clearly makes it impossible for people of different faiths to get married. The burden of proof that they have not committed a cognizable offence is squarely on them.

The criminalizing of conversions had happened many decades ago, with even non-BJP governments bringing in laws that inserted the state into the relationship of people with their maker. So missionaries or Muslim clerics could be easily accused of using force, coercion, allurement, deceit and fraud could be charged under laws which in many states are now non-bailable and cognizable offences. The ground had already been prepared over decades by taking a hostile view of conversions. Now, the state police have been given unbridled powers to investigate matters of change of faith: a police officer need not have a warrant to arrest a suspect and needs no court permissions to start investigations.[4] So citizens can change jobs, aspire to change nationalities, but not exercise agency when it comes to a deeply personal question of faith. Complaints can be filed by a blood relation, in-laws, adopted relatives of the person seeking to convert and any person involved in assisting the process can be booked under the law.

The law has penalties for imprisonment between one and five years and a penalty of Rs 15,000 and above. Where a minor girl or a woman from the Scheduled Caste or Scheduled Tribe communities is deemed as the 'victim', jailtime could be from three to ten years and a penalty of not less than Rs 25,000.

The law provides for rendering a marriage seen to be one solemnized to convert the girl as void. The burden of proof is on the defendant. The law has built in a verification process, wherein to change one's faith, a person will have to apply to the district magistrate, two months in advance of the marriage. This is twice the period the 1954 Special Marriage Act lays down. The affidavits are detailed and must have names of both parents, permanent address, current address, age, sex, occupation, marital status, monthly income, dependents, caste status, the faith one is converting to and details of who is performing the conversion. The magistrate, on receiving this application, has the power to order a police inquiry to check the 'real intention, purpose and cause' of conversion.

In the second stage, the applicant needs to send a separate affidavit to the magistrate within sixty days of the conversion. The magistrate will then display a notice for twenty-one days to invite objections, after which the conversion can be confirmed.

But this new law is also veiled patriarchy. The government claims that the law was needed to protect women from men luring them or committing fraud.

This disingenuous reason, given with a straight face, of protecting Hindu women from men brazenly reveals the deeper reasons why Hindu women being married to Muslim men provokes a deep anxiety, while the opposite is openly welcomed. So, patriarchy, where women need rescuing, but from only the Muslim man, locks in this very attractive principle with large sections of Indian men already threatened by Indian women looking to expand their freedoms over the last few decades. This new law, formulated supposedly as a response to the so-called 'Love Jihad' bogey, allows control over personal choices of women, claiming to protect them, while in reality further circumscribing their worlds.

Scholar Charu Gupta has studied how this is not new, but the stoking of fears which were set alight as early as the 1920s. This is also fulfilling the agenda of what was desired then: to put a stop to female autonomy and blacklist the Muslim man. According to her, 'Inter-religious love and marriages are a tricky terrain. They challenge various norms and customs and arouse passions of religious fundamentalists. The "threat" of such intimacies has often resulted in "constructed" campaigns, expressing the anxieties and fears of conservative forces.' She writes that as a historian:

> One is struck by the uncanny resemblance of the issue and its language to similar 'abduction' and conversion campaigns launched by the Arya Samaj and other Hindu revivalist bodies in the 1920s in north India, to draw sharper lines between Hindus and Muslims. Seen through the prism of a historical perspective, the dichotomy and falseness of the allegations of the Hindu

right appear more starkly. It also points to how certain tropes have been deployed repeatedly in different circumstances by Hindu groups, where the body of the Hindu woman has become a site for both claims to community homogeneity and honour, as well as for cracks within its articulation.

In the 1920s, militant Hindu assertion reached new heights, especially in the context of shuddhi (purification movement to reclaim those who had converted from Hinduism to other religions) and sangathan (organization in defence of Hindu interests) movements launched by the Arya Samaj. This period saw increased and unprecedented communal clashes in Uttar Pradesh. What is significant in the present context is that in this period the Hindu woman's body became a marker to sharpen communal boundaries in ways more aggressive than before. The period witnessed a flurry of orchestrated propaganda campaigns and popular inflammatory and demagogic appeals by a section of Hindu publicists and the Arya Samaj against abductions and conversions of Hindu women by Muslim goondas, ranging from allegations of rape, abduction and elopement, to luring, conversion, love and forced marriages. Drawing on diverse sources like newspapers, pamphlets, meetings, handbills, posters, novels, myths, rumours and gossip, the campaign was able to operate in a public domain, and monopolise

> the field of everyday representation. Abductions and conversions of Hindu women by Muslims became one of the main determinants of Hindu identity and consciousness in the period, providing Hindu publicists with a common reference point. The abducted and converted Hindu woman was metamorphosed into a symbol of both sacredness and humiliation, and hence of the victimisation of the whole Hindu community. Allegations of abductions caused a number of localised affrays, and even occasional riot, for example in Kanpur in June 1924 and in Mathura in March 1928, where it was reported that a Muslim man had eloped with a Hindu woman.[5]

The utterance of 'talaq, talaq, talaq' has been struck down by the Supreme Court as not being a legal method of divorce. Yet, when Muslim men utter these now meaningless words, it is a criminal offence! If the same words are uttered by men of another faith, they are not a criminal offence. To my mind, the inference of this being discriminatory towards men of a certain faith is a logical one.

❧

The new laws outlining what 'new' India is—a peeling back from what was a diverse, varied and unique attempt at building a multi-identity nation in 1947—will not be stopped by a few odd inter-faith marriages taking place. But the existence of shared spaces which allowed the final frontier of who you will marry to be breached, and that this was facilitated by the state, was a signal about who the Indian state was and what the Indian state aspired to be. What is spoken of as constitutional values, whether it is Article 14 or 19, the right to be equal or free has never been realized perfectly or completely by all Indians; only a fool would suggest that. Social values or what was practised in homes or even privately, semi-publicly, had rarely been in sync with universal rights that the Indian Constitution guarantees. But the Indian state, by standing where it did, signalled the kind of society India aspired to be in order to be able to uplift its millions and afford them each dignity.

It is in this context that the Special Marriages Act, 1954, was truly special and needed protecting. Like a canary in a coalmine, what happens to inter-faith couples and what is sought to be done unto them by the arm of the law is a summary of what those who bring these laws think about the idea of coexistence or of the principle of equal rights for all Indians.

Anees and Sumitra should be the stuff of audacious romantic novels, but these kinds of stories end up in the dock in India today; and this speaks to the value of love, the value of women that those making these laws have.

As their daughter, I had hoped, fervently so, to never feel the need to tell their story and reveal details they would have baulked at sharing publicly when alive. But I have crossed that rubicon and been forced to lend words to characterizing the sentiment that bound them and to elaborate on personal details of the world they created. Only because it is important to speak today of the world that was possible in India, where the idea of India was not just an 'idea' idea but a lived reality. Even if part of the larger, sometimes ugly and broken, mosaic of what constituted how India lived, Anees and Sumitra's kitchen, home, life and ideals are an important testament. They are a testament to their courage, love, fearlessness and ability to imagine and write their own stories. Their togetherness is a testament to how by breaking both the visible and invisible chains that their respective 'societies' would have bound them by, they managed to create a very different reality from what others around them would have wanted them to live by.

But beyond that, too, Anees and Sumitra are a product of their times. Their story is an ode to all that made their coming together possible, emphasized and underlined fraternity. Together, they forced you to see beyond the shackles of petty prejudice and biases all communities or social groups live with.

When Anees and Sumitra got together and planned to stay together, it cemented many ideas of India into one. That is the reason I have been compelled to tell the story of that India, through the story of my parents meeting, marrying and settling, even though they were fiercely protective of each other and their privacy and would never have dreamt of articulating it publicly, let alone printing it. Of course, the story of an India of confluence has met with challenges before 2014 too, but it faces its biggest challenge so far with a new and increasingly bitter narrative of division and otherness being spun and being written into laws. It was most starkly described in slow detail to us by Prime Minister Narendra Modi in UP in 2017, via the difference between a shamshan and qabristan. Sumitra died in 2005 and Anees in 2018. As one who laid each of her parents to rest, one in a shamshan and another in a qabristan, I can testify that it felt exactly the same.

This short book is a tribute to all that came before their last journeys and the big promise of India they brought into their modest home. For it is in these stories, and countless others like theirs and the lives that they in turn touched, that the Indian Constitution becomes the guiding light which ensures that we keep our eyes set on higher ideals, to achieve more togetherness, liberty, equality and much more of fraternity.

One

Sumitra

It was 1933 and India was under British rule. Dr Dhan Singh was a reputed physician in the town of Arsikere, then in Chikmagalur district (now a part of Hassan district), whom several influential people relied on for his 'combination' medicines, prescriptions and advice. On 5 December 1933, the doctor's wife, Shivana Bai, gave birth to their daughter Sumitra, their twelfth child. Dhan Singh and Shivana Bai's was an unusual union in those days—a Vaishnavite man and his Shaivite wife. South India had seen that as an embittered line of division for a long time and it was hard to bridge.

Sumitra and her mother remained at their ancestral home after Dhan Singh's death when Sumitra was just five years old. Shivana had many children (twelve surviving and at least two born after Sumitra who died in early infancy). With so many who had died in childbirth, she was very protective of those who had lived on. As a child, Sumitra found herself somewhat insecure and yet determined to fight her circumstances from the very start. She grew up with a stern and often punishing sister-in-law who made her do all the housework and was fixated on getting her hitched early on in life so the 'burden' could be relieved. Through her many chores, she managed to discover a love for reading and books, convinced that her destiny lay elsewhere and not as a submissive wife to the elderly man whose proposal her sister-in-law was contemplating. She confided in me much later that it was under an open sky, in the washrooms then prevalent in Indian homes, that she had first dared to dream of going away as far as she could to study and travel.

It was 1942 and a troubled time for India, and for the girl in Arsikere. Sumitra's older brothers, D. Shankar Singh and D. Anant Singh, were drawn to Gandhi and the Quit India movement, and even served prison sentences during the freedom struggle. She would later recall visiting them in jail and singing '*Vijayi vishwa tiranga pyara, jhanda ooncha rahe humara*', scurrying away when the jailer chased them.

Her beloved brother Shankar, who was thirteen years older, had his own plans besides freeing India from the British. Drawn irresistibly to the moving image, at the time a new technology with tremendous potential, he had moved to Mysore, sold his two touring talkies—Gandhi Talkies and Nehru Talkies—and was keen to enter film production. On one of his visits back home, Sumitra, under the guise of pouring water to wash his hands after a meal, got hold of her brother and confided in him that she had been told she would have to drop out of school and get married. 'I just want to read and study, Papanna, please take me away. I just do housework here and struggle to find time to do other things.'

The year was 1948 and, without losing a moment, Papannna, or Shankar, brought his mother and youngest sister to Mysore where they lived in a large home with his wife, children and at least four other relatives whom he helped financially and emotionally. The journey to Mysore as a young girl, to class eight of its Christ the King School, was a dream come true for Sumitra. Independence from British rule for India had coincided with her being given the freedom to make something of her life and do well. Her own mother, Shivana Bai, was a woman of exceptional intelligence, she recalled, albeit completely illiterate. She continued to support Sumitra's desire to not be locked up. Her father had left considerable money and jewels for her marriage, but Shivana was unable to secure that back from her eldest son. She was able to pass on her very substantial jewel worn around her neck and a cummerbund to Sumitra. But Shivana fell very sick a few years after coming to Mysore. Sumitra's brother was doing well in the film world, his Kannada movie *Jagan Mohini* was a big hit, earning him acclaim and fame and also enabling him to make a lot of money, which he was very generous with. There were yards of fabric bought for the entire family, and stacks of Mysore silk saris that he would distribute at home as evenly as he could. Shivana Bai died soon after the release of his hit film, and Shankar Singh gave her a grand farewell, determined to protect Sumitra, under his care, even more. Small gestures, which were not so small for Sumitra—like a table lamp so she could study at night without disturbing anyone else—were lifelines that made her later journey possible.

In Mysore, her brother's success in the Kannada film world as a producer and director of repute suddenly threw open the world of glamour around Sumitra—cine-talk, grand sets, shooting schedules, camera angles, the socializing and get-togethers. After completing her school examinations, she was made to accompany her sister-in-law, Pratima Devi, an actress in her own right, to Madras on a shoot and there she got a closer look at this mesmerizing world of fame and glamour. But it only served to increase Sumitra's restlessness to get away and do some more reading and writing and understand the world around her.

A brilliant student, she consistently did well and decided to pursue economics at Maharani's College, University of Mysore. Aware of the fees her brother was paying and no longer wanting to be a burden on him,

Sumitra chased every scholarship with determination. Pratima Devi recalls how she would line up to get her marksheets certified and make a case for all scholarships that were available. She topped the university in economics in her BA programme, becoming the first woman to do so. But that did not create as much of a stir in the faculty as the fact that she was a non-Brahmin. My mother would recall how her kind but shocked teachers came to her house to check for themselves that she was a Kshatriya, not a Brahmin! The graded inequities of the caste system had visited my mother's consciousness before this as well. She had told me about when she was scolded and given a mud bath after having eaten at the home of a classmate who was the daughter of a shoemaker. The anger Sumitra had felt as she was instructed to 'purify' herself went some way in making her who she was and seeking flight from home at the first opportunity. Delhi seemed an exciting prospect at the time, a city considered very far those days, a city where she could be different and not have to explain herself all the time or have her life interrupted by either mud baths or teachers who came home to measure just how 'high-born' she was.

The capital city had many established and burgeoning institutes, and she was sure a doctorate is what she wanted to pursue. So under economist Dr Sukhamoy

Chakravarty, she wrote her thesis on the terms of trade between India and East Europe which was also published as her first book in 1973. But that was not enough for her. Her mother had left her an expensive piece of jewellery, an heirloom that she sold to complete her post-doctorate at the International Institute of Social Studies, The Hague, in the Netherlands.

Her time in the Netherlands, complete with the ship journey and the global cast of students she met there, opened her mind to the world and life beyond Indian shores. It was a post-World War world, where the peace dividend was kicking in and Sumitra truly benefitted from sharing life experiences with her new-found Italian and Hungarian friends. She learnt to make the goulash and it sealed her conversion to a cosmopolitanism that had always been part of her personality. Being mindful of her circumstances, her beginnings in Arsikere and how she had got there on her own initiative ensured that she remained committed to why she was there. Books, libraries, what separated the developed world from poor countries and why it should not always stay that way preoccupied her senses. Upon her return to Delhi, she found herself a job at the Indian Institute of Foreign Trade, then housed in a small building in south Delhi's Green Park. But that was still not all that she did—plugged into the larger story of India and determined to contribute to ideas, criticism and the building of the young nation, her work with a variety of magazines and journals, sometimes attributed to her and sometimes not, helped her pursue her dream of being able to push ideas and contribute towards the direction that India must evolve in.

Sumitra ended up travelling well beyond the little town of Arsikere and Mysore and became the 'Delhi phupphu' or 'Delhi ajji' to her younger relatives back home. The whiff of jasmine, the backyard conversations in Mysore, the reassurance that her brother Shankar was always at hand never left Sumitra. She did not leave Mysore either. Her ashes made their way into the Cauvery, just off Srirangapatnam, in 2005. Each year, a gold medal in her name is awarded to the student securing the highest grades in the final year of BA (economics) in Maharani's College.

Two

Anees

In distant Uttar Pradesh, as the nation awakened to a new dawn, seven-year-old Anees lay confined to the bed down with a serious bout of typhoid. It was only towards the end of 1947 that he somehow recovered, returning, it felt, 'almost from the jaws of death'. My father Anees Chishti's notes, discovered posthumously, describe his childhood—witness to the immediate aftermath of Partition for a prominent Muslim family that had proudly decided to stay on in Deoria, in the newly independent India.

Anees was born on 12 October 1940 in a kuchha house near the railway tracks of the Oudh Tirhut Railway or OTR (later North Eastern Railway) that connected Lucknow with Katihar.

One memory etched in his memory, 'as if it were only yesterday', was of huge crowds gathering in the small town's street in 1948 to catch a glimpse of the urn containing the ashes of Mahatma Gandhi, brought from Delhi following his assassination on 30 January (perhaps to be immersed in the River Sarayu at Barhaj, only 18 miles from Deoria).

The Chishti family of Deoria in the present state of Uttar Pradesh traces its roots to the time when three brothers migrated to this small town that was a tehsil of the Gorakhpur district, sometime around 1860, from the town of Machchlishehar in Jaunpur district. My grandfather Syed Mohammad Chishti (popularly known as Nanhey Chishti) was a successful lawyer—the first advocate in the family of legal practitioners having graduated from Aligarh Muslim University (AMU)—and a popular social figure.

At the time of Partition, Anees's father had a fairly good practice as a lawyer in Deoria and they had a comfortable family life. In his notes, my father writes about the pre-Partition anxiety among Muslim families, including his own: '...the decision of whether to stay in the land of our ancestors or to migrate to the newly created country of Pakistan which was expected to offer better job opportunities and brighter prospects. Where there would not be any prejudice or ill-feeling and jealousy against people like my father for reasons of religion or the backlash of the country's partition. Every evening there were discussions behind closed doors as to whether to leave the country for a land of our co-religionists or stay back in the hope that good sense would prevail over people from both communities and there would be harmony and cordiality after hostilities die down.'

My father escaped life as a possible engineer when he ran away, absenting himself from an engineering entrance examination at AMU which his father was keen Anees sit for. He had an instinct for the liberal arts, but ended up settling for statistics, as a compromise with his father. He completed his MSc in it but never really enjoyed his subject, per se. But life in AMU had a lot to offer. He found friends; his elder brother, an aspiring poet, Ahsan Chishti, too was a senior. The poet Shahryar was present too, and AMU, with its famed mehfils, sessions and bright students, provided an ambience and nursery for his reading to widen and his mind to grow. Café d' Phoos—a café with a thatched roof—Aligarh's famous bakeries with their paape, the market and Aligarh's numaaish, all figured in our conversations at home long after he had completed his stint at the university. He met his very dear friend and room partner, the bio-chemist Prof. Habibul Haque, who went on to become one of his lifelong friends, and the hockey player Ali Sayeed, who was part of the Indian team that won the gold medal at the Tokyo Olympics in 1964. All of them developed a sharp interest in sports, world affairs, literature, art, culture, and aesthetics. AMU's zeitgeist, its wry sense of humour and the proud fraternity it forged between students and with some teachers remained a part of life even after they all graduated and left the campus.

Even though the eastern part of the then United Provinces had not seen any killings or even demonstrations of extreme hostility between Hindus and Muslims, horrible stories were trickling in from areas affected by communal riots, and Anees's family, too, was gripped by fear of possible deterioration in the communal situation in the days to come.

Anees's father, who was forty at the time of Partition, had a distinguished record of graduate and law studies at AMU: he had topped the LLB examination and been awarded the university medal. The student who came in second belonged to a neighbouring town. He tried to convince Anees's father that the future of Muslims in a divided India was going to be disheartening and it would be better to migrate to Pakistan where he could expect to secure a good position in the new legal system. But, as Anees writes, 'my father—who was greatly involved in the social life of our small town and had immense faith in people around him—had different ideas and stood his ground in the hope that in a few years the environment of the country would be harmonious and cordial. He chose diversity against a rather monotonous uniformity of cultures and ways of life.' His family was a Syed Muslim, one which had come to Deoria to, in all probability, escape the attention of the British for its role in Ghadar in 1857 from Jaunpur in East Uttar Pradesh. Anees's father became a leading advocate in Deoria and his family was one that valued modern education and the arts. Two of his sisters were studying music.

'Significantly enough, the idea of migrating to Pakistan did not find favour with the elders of my own generation,' Anees continues. 'Among my cousins and close relatives, only two brothers, Masood Bhai and Naseem Bhai, who had a fairly good academic record at Allahabad University, chose to go over to Pakistan with the hope of finding good employment and they both succeeded in their missions. Masood Bhai was absorbed in the information structure of the government and rose to become the director of the Lahore station of Radio Pakistan, and Naseem Bhai became a senior officer at a leading bank of the country.'

Despite the fact that the family was respected by members of both communities in the town and had very good relations with the officials of the government machinery, some unsettling incidents did take place that were unsavoury and foretold the many battles that remained to be waged to ensure genuine equality for India's largest minority.

Here is an entry from the diary he kept during those days:

We had a big Twin gramophone in the house, perhaps of late thirties' vintage. We had a good collection of records, both classical Hindustani music as well as popular songs from Hindi films—by Noor Jehan, Pankaj Mullick, Malika Pukhraj and other pre-Lata Mangeshkar–Rafi/ Mukesh era singers. We used to play these records in our moments of relaxation and when other relatives and family friends visited us. It was kept in a room whose window opened out to the narrow lane that led to the pond behind our house. It was deserted and rarely anyone passed through it, particularly in the evenings. We came to know that some 'mukhbir' (informant) of the intelligence department had reported to the higher authorities that in our house there was a transmitter and very often several people were sitting surrounding it and probably speaking in low voices that were not audible fact the lane besides the window and the matter needed some investigation.

The official to whom this apprehension was reported had a hearty laugh. It turned out he was well aware of the music sessions around the Twin gramophone, having been an occassional participant himself. The whole incident was laughed off. But when we later thought about it, we couldn't help wonder … what if the official did not know the family and a probe had actually been ordered? The fear from our minds had not yet entirely gone!

While we lived under the shadow of fear and lack of firm belief in the decision the family had taken to stay back in India rejecting what most members of the Muslim community at that point of time believed was the good life and security that awaited them in the new country of Pakistan, there were some very positive factors that gave us the confidence that we had made the right decision of living in a country that had a plural society with multiplicity of religious groups that were living in harmony for centuries in a spirit of inclusiveness instead of going over to a new nation carved our solely on the basis of religious separation and a craving for exclusivity. An imagined uniformity of culture and religion was given up in favour of an existing unity in diversity, a unity that had temporarily developed cracks due to the machinations of the country's foreign rulers resulting in an atmosphere of hatred and intolerance. The cracks were bound to disappear with the passage of time. This was the belief that had prompted us to take a decision to stay where we were, despite the stories that we used to hear of some of the town's Muslims, even some who were not very well educated who found themselves very gainfully employed in Pakistan, something they could not expect in India, they felt.

Our faith, in the spirit of mutual trust between the people of the town was strengthened on the occasions when this trust came to be on trial. If there were harrowing incidents and narrow escapes there were some heartening moments too, when the family's faith in the people of the town was strengthened.

At the height of trouble, it was rumoured that something was brewing and some Muslim families may come under attack. Our neighbour, Thakur Kamla Singh, a respected lawyer, a product of Banaras Hindu University, who had excelled in wrestling during his study for the Law Degree, was a close friend of my father. When he came to hear about these 'rumours', he lost no time, as he had returned from the court, and came to our house with a very strong lathi and asked us for a chair to be brought from inside the house. He sat in the chair and made it known to the people around that he would be sitting outside the house for the whole night, if necessary, and whomsoever dared to bring any harm to our family would have to encounter him before anyone else is touched. He was a very respectable citizen and he was joined by many others to demonstrate solidarity with the fairly he had chosen to guard in an environment of tension and raised passions. This was enough to send the right signals to the miscreants who might have been planning to create trouble. As a result, nothing disturbing happened in any part of the town and Thakur Kamla Singh's message had gone down to the people. Everyone felt relieved and we slept well at night after thanking Thakur Sahib for his very noble sentiments and the brave act that became a symbol of solidarity and mutual warmth between people of different communities. Some similar cases of show of solidarity and trust were reported from some other parts of the town as well. We never heard of any threats or show of hatred or malice from any section of the society. We felt proud of the age-old harmony and cordiality around us.

What Thakur Kamla Singh did on that evening of tension and suspicion may seem a minor expression of mutual trust between two friendly families. But it had a much deeper effect and became the cause of confidence and re-assurance for a minority of less than five percent in the town. Goodwill had triumphed over ill will. Inclusiveness had served over exclusiveness.

Anees's life—as a curious and interested young person who was able to procure the Calcutta edition of *The Statesman* in the small town of Deoria; familiarize himself with Amrita Sher-Gil and modern art and culture burgeoning in India; read Shakespeare, Mir and Ghalib—was as much a testimony to his varied interests and unique mind as it was to the cosmopolitanism that marked life in a very small town of UP. The government school, which he started attending only when nine years old, and his home tutoring provided a well-rounded view, something which may be hard to say about the same town today.

A Nephew Remembers

Shahid Amin

My first memory of Anees mamun is of being taken to the Government School, Deoria, in July 1960. I had come through class four, or what was called J-2 in our well-endowed New Delhi school. We were a privileged lot: the school boasted of a swimming pool and half a dozen horses with names like Diana for seniors to ride and tent-peg. But things were about to change: my father was leaving for the US for two years; the family was to shift to our ancestral home in eastern Uttar Pradesh.

It fell to the lot of Anees mamun to convince me that K.E. Ucchatar Madhyamik Vidyalaya—formerly King Edward Government School—would be as good for me as it had been for mamun and his lawyer father, who had famously travelled the 250 miles to watch Sobers, the

West Indian all-rounder, miss a double century at Kanpur in 1958.

Anees loved the game. He also founded the Chishti XI, which played both on its home ground, a portion of which was lost to the arhar dal crop at the peak of the cricket season, and toured small towns with such names as Bhatni and Bhatpar Rani, down the metre gauge railway track. A cricket aficionado, he was equally passionate about hockey. Jubilee School, in neighbouring Gorakhpur, had been the breeding ground of such hockey internationals as the brilliant left-in Inam-ur-Rahman and his dribbling partner on the flank Ali Sayeed, both of whom remained Anees mamun's lifelong friends. The pride of place in the drawing room of his house in south Delhi was held by the battered hockey ball which the victorious AMU team had signed and gifted him after beating a strong Punjab side at the varsity final. To everyone's regret, Zainab, the domestic worker, had inadvertently scrubbed the ball 'dirtied' by all those signatures clean.

As an undergraduate at Aligarh, Anees had already begun taking newspapers seriously. He must have scoured intently *The Statesman*, for over the summers he returned to Deoria with stacks of the Delhi edition, getting these bound in trimonthly volumes. I so wish mamun had brought these back to Delhi; for one, on its sports pages was a full report of Delhi University's 1959 win over a test-material Bombay XI. The cream-coloured stump that Inderjitsinhji—who went on to keep wickets for India—had gifted me as a souvenir would have served as a prologue to the tale of the cricket buff-statistician-journalist Anees Chishti.

In the year 1961, *Chishti Times* came out from Deoria. A four-page broadsheet, it appeared twice during the summer holidays when the extended family was at its full strength. Its logo mimicked the old-style italic font that *The Statesman* and other leading newspapers used at the time; its stories, three columns to a page in mamun's immaculate hand, were largely about familial issues: an upcoming marriage in Sultanpur, the sacrificial goat taking ill before Bakrid; and national matters, such as the long run of *Mughal-e-Azam* in Gorakhpur.

I think it was the summer of 1962 when mamun came to stay with us in Delhi. My father had a spacious bungalow in the St. Stephen's College campus, opposite the College Chapel. Anees had joined the Pusa Agricultural Institute as a statistician and had a room in the R block of New Rajinder Nagar, which was the end point of a newly started bus service, quaintly called no. 4A. His small library at our house had such authors as Sukhatme and issues of the ISI journal *Sankhya*, but he was already seeking a niche in the small literary sphere of the city. One of the earlier pieces he wrote was an astringent review of V.S. Naipaul's *An Area of Darkness* (1964), I think, for *Mainstream*. Anees mamun knew the Gorakhpur of Naipaul's ancestors well, as he was familiar with the English-educated elites of cities like Delhi who were the object of Naipaul's biting ire.

This opening salvo, so to speak, against a fellow Gorakhpuria was followed by a steady stream of cultural pieces. Reviews of dance performances (Yamini Krishnamurthy and Indrani Rahman), the plays of Alkazi and Yatrik, appreciation of the Shankar-Shad Mushairas, where the top poets of Indo-Pak, as the phrase went, came together every winter.

Anees mamun's columns were now a regular feature in *Mainstream* and *Shankar's Weekly*. Mamun was deeply involved in the affairs of Nikhil Chakravarty's weekly magazine, *Mainstream*. Soon, Romesh Thapar took him under his wings and made room for him as assistant editor for *Seminar*. Anees, who remembered Romesh Thapar as 'Bani Master', the elder brother of the struggling journalist Dilip Kumar of Zia Sarhadi's *Footpath* (1953), now joined hands with the Thapars to bring out some memorable issues of the magazine. 'Academic Colonialism' and 'Secularism in Crisis' stick in mind. He invited his friend

O.V. Vijayan, the brilliant cartoonist and latter-day master of Malayali fiction, to contribute, and introduced Chand Joshi, the student radical from Delhi University, to the world of letters.

In 1965, or perhaps late 1964, Anees met Sumitra who was finishing her PhD in International Trade at Sapru House, the watering hole for researchers and journalists at Barakhamba Road, adjacent to my school. Mamun, still with us at St. Stephen's, would leave fairly early in the morning and come back at dinner time—he was courting Mumani. I came to know about this 'development', as it was termed in our traditional middle-class family, from Zoya, Sheila Sandhu's daughter, who used to stand behind me during the morning prayers in school. (Sheila Sandhu was a brilliant publisher who reinvented Rajkamal Prakashan and was a generous patron of writers and artists.) They married in a small ceremony at our house: the bride's party consisted of Sheilaji, friends Rajni and Hayat from Sapru House; and the Amin family made up the groom's party. We were invited to 18, Ring Road, Lajpat Nagar, Sheila Sandhu's posh house with a swimming pool, for the wedding reception—still fresh in my memory for the juicy tandoori chicken which I was savouring for the first time and the car ride home via the newly built Ring Road. The Chishtis then moved into a barsati in C block, Defence Colony.

A sidekick for long, I had by now graduated to being a proper acolyte. Names of books, authors, sportsmen: Sudhir Dhar, Subhadra Joshi, G.P. Deshpande, Ali Sayeed (Anees Mamun's friend who gifted me the official souvenir of Tokyo Olympics); *The Yogi and the Commissar*, *Ghost in the Machine*, *The Medium is the Message*, *Beyond a Boundary*, cybernetics! (Mamun had published two articles on the history of computation), Kenneth Clark's *The Nude* (how I wish I hadn't let go of it), Raja Rao's *The Serpent and the Rope*—I gave up after a few pages—*Myth of Sisyphus* (I retain the hardback edition), hockey matches at the stadium near Gol Market, Ranji Trophy at Kotla, DCM and Durand at the Delhi Gate … Anees mamun surprising 'Firaq' with a request to autograph an advance copy of *Gul-e-Naghma* after the Gyanpeeth ceremony … I sharing the partitioned sitting room for the night with the great Nushur Wahidi on return from the Mushaira. … Mumani using the Urdu word 'atraaf' while sprinkling ghee on to south Indian vegetable pulao with a circular motion … the Amins alighting from no. 29 at Sant Nagar, trudging across the then barren ground to E-73, Greater Kailash. … Mumani, gravid with Seema, alone with me at our house—the rest of the family had to rush off to Deoria—advising me to read Samuelson's *Economics* in addition to the textbook … I getting 55/100 in the Higher Secondary in my favourite subject …

returning with Anees mamun to Delhi in 1962, staying at the Naaz Hotel in Jama Masjid, tucking into 'Chicken Jahangiri'—a novelty—at Flora, failing the entrance exam for readmission to Modern School.

This was all sixty years ago. Looking back, Anees Chishti was a blend of being, belonging and thinking that we all cherished and seem to have lost for some time now.

Three

'Just Good Friends'

My parents were as different as they could be; their regional, religious and age differences were compounded by the fact that she was well-settled by the time they met and he was struggling to be a journalist and aspiring to be a writer.

But as he set his gaze upon the cotton saree-clad 'thin and wheatish' Dr D. Sumitra Bai at the basement office of *Mainstream* in Connaught Place, New Delhi, Mohammed Anees Chishti experienced a surge in emotions that he could not immediately explain to himself. The girl he had just met could not be more different from him in terms of background. But he experienced a fellowship that the shy Anees later firmly put down as the first signs of a powerful attraction that brought them together and would surmount any worldly differences.

My mother had told me she was first struck by Anees's quietude, and a sense that still waters ran deep. His warm and comforting handshake is something that stayed with her. The office was small and the first meeting was fleeting,

I cannot confirm if they even shared a cup of tea at that meeting or if Anees just dropped his article and went away. But for both, it appears to have been an important one which each of them recalled to me as special and memorable.

Anees was on a fellowship at the Pusa Institute of Agriculture, but wanted to desperately shake off the shackles that a post-graduation in statistics meant.

She felt an inexorable draw to the left by the time she met Anees. When Anees, deeply influenced by ornithologist Salim Ali at the time, struck up a conversation around bird-watching, Sumitra could not help sneering and said, 'What a bourgeois preoccupation.' Anees agreed and said, 'Yes, that is what it is, but it has its uses,' and continued to talk about birds.

But they were similar too in ways that had crept upon them once they started meeting. They shared deep political and social commitments, spoke of the poor and empathized with them in ways that did not get covered by any theory. This gave them both the language to speak and reach out to each other despite other seemingly unbridgeable gaps. They were thinking individuals, both wrote for the progressive magazine *Mainstream*. Sumitra played a key part and assisted its editor, Nikhil Chakravarty; she ghostwrote vast portions, in addition to signed pieces. Anees wrote mostly under his name. Both were committed to getting the magazine off the ground each week. This they both recalled as being the closest to a shared religious ritual.

Anees and Sumitra set out as friends, later good friends, sharing interests, passions and commitments in an India where this small middle class, which they represented, in its various towns was slowly beginning to emerge, getting to know each other, across state and spatial boundaries. This lot of English-knowing but small-town persons, brought together through education, employment and ideas evolving in India, met in its cities and were a part of its slowly blossoming urbanism.

The 1960s were a time of uncertainty. The immediate rush and high of Independence was over and while optimism still reigned, it was tinged with strong shades of doubt too. Institutions were being built but had not quite blossomed and there was a certain promise about India in parts but a reality check too about the tough path forward.

Interpersonal spaces were also invaded by the politics and society of the day. The '60s after the death of Jawaharlal Nehru was also a time of turmoil. Socially, while romantic associations now are sought to be criminalized by law, it was not as if then they had social sanction. Anees and Sumitra were familiar with huge changes in terms of gender and social relationships that were taking place in the world, but India was still conservative. If not the police, there was always the fear that friends and family would not stand by free choices exercised by individuals. They both moved in progressive circles but hailed from such diverse backgrounds, oceans apart, that they both treaded cautiously, tip-toeing around each other in matters of the heart.

They were careful around imagined boundaries of the other, so as to not appear too 'forward', first gauging and feeling around what the other would find acceptable. Anees, not quite sure of what kind of relationship Sumitra expected, decided to test-drive with that old staple, a movie: *The Householder*, in which Romesh Thapar, a dynamic journalist, the man behind the First Amendment to the Constitution, plays a part. The theatre was Delhi's Rivoli, and Anees loved Ruth Praver Jhabvala's writing and Romesh Thapar too. Sumitra went along, and this, in 1964, was a signal to Anees that she would not be averse to getting to know him better, in ways not necessarily as 'just' friends. It was a test-drive, and it worked.

Anees shared his thoughts about writing the IAS exam with international law as a subject and Sumitra was happy to help him with a copy of a key book on it she had, *Starke's International Law*. He noted her name inscribed on it, he read the Sumitra Bai scrawl as 'Sumitra

Daj' and was confused, wondering if she was Rajasthani, then how did the Mysore connection add up? But it did not matter. Those were the days when you just bought a book, not books.

Anees used to be the dance and theatre critic for *Shankar's Weekly* then, a very sought-after magazine. He also got innumerable passes for theatre and classical dance events each week, and would take his precious Sumitra to those, for free. His reviews gave him Rs 15 a piece.

Both Anees and Sumitra were anything but upper class. It was about first-generation migrants with minimal resources trying to pitch their tent in a hot and not very friendly city.

Sumitra was better networked at the time, with friends very close to the Communist Party, and shared their dreams, persuasions and hopes for a better India. Anees leaned left too, but was not quite in with the same crowd, and preferred to keep his distance.

But, slowly and surely, they started moving around together, seeing art, films, even watching the Ranji Trophy match at the Ferozeshah Kotla maidan, something that Sumitra certainly did not relish.

Their relationship was still not quite open, though it was not hidden either. They took their time coming to terms with it in their own ways. How must anyone be told about this? Should someone be informed other than their close circle of friends and should families at all be drawn in at this time? Could they be trusted to understand their sense of fellowship, comfort and attraction? For one, Sumitra was eight years older. How would Anees's family take it? Neither believed in any gods or God, but did not believe in flaunting their disbelief or doubts either. Those were quieter times and they felt little need to speak of gods or avowals of faith.

Anees recalled how riots in the early 1960s, in Jabalpur, Rourkela and Sagar, had shaken Muslims in faraway UP. The Sino–Indian war in 1962 added another dimension to the uncertainty, and Nehru's death, he said, delivered a stunning blow. Significant sections of Muslims saw Nehru as a saviour—what kind of India would take shape after the death of such a vocal advocate of secularism dominated hushed conversations in many Muslim homes.

Anees recalled how in an article for *Mainstream* on the danseuse Yamini Krishnamurthi, he had ended with a tailpiece on his experience at Puri, when, as a student, he had been very keen to go to the Jagannath Temple, but having seen the board outside restricting entry for Muslims, he had not ventured in. Sumitra, while proofreading the piece, was perturbed and disbelieving, until a fellow editor at *Mainstream* told her that the ban on non-Hindus did indeed exist, and was only one of the many ugly leftover battles for India to wage before it could truly claim inclusivity and equality for its citizens.

In the 1960 student elections at AMU, no Hindus had been elected, and that was the first time this had happened (usually there was some representation). The poll in-charge made some inflammatory comments making it sound like a good thing. Riots broke out in the city. Students at the university stayed quiet, except for rioting at a bookshop and scattering books. It was Anees's favourite bookshop—Singhal's—and when he saw the Quran lying around, he picked it up, anxious that it not fuel further resentment. He ended up gifting the book to Jasbir, his footballer roommate, a turbanned Sikh, to escape the charge that it was 'stolen goods'.

As they all returned home in batches, Anees recalled the fear they had of being attacked once the train crossed Aligarh, distinct as they were in their black sherwanis. But then, he added, 'Jasbir was travelling with us. He was our leader. We were sure we were safe in the train as long as Jasbir was with us.'

Even in their youth, both my parents were untouched by personal prejudice. My mother, being from the south, had not experienced the trauma of Partition quite as closely as north India had. No doubt families migrated from south India too, but the heat of Partition that hit the northern, western Indian states and Bengal was of another order. Most Hindu refugees from Pakistan had settled in north India, where the wound and the hurt festered for long. South India was not haunted by the break in 1947 in quite the same way. But she was learning about sharper Hindu–Muslim divides that she sensed prevailed in north India. She learnt about those slowly, asking Anees, discussing things and sharing experiences with him. Mostly, it was their own belief in what they shared that had got them started and that kept them going. Their confidence in their shared spirit and expectations of what the future held, despite all that ostensibly kept them apart, was the glue that joined them.

Their names, oddly enough, things that they had not chosen but their families had, brought them together. 'Anees' and 'Sumitra' mean the same thing, Anees in Arabic and Sumitra in Sanskrit translate as 'good friends'. It was one more thing that was common to them. If they'd been believers, they would have read it as a sign.

'Qubool hai!', vermillion, jasmine flowers, bindi and Bakrid

In the wake of the 1965 Indo–Pakistan war, Delhi was a tense place. The soldiers were settling scores on the border, but civilians too were feeling the heat. Tension spilled over into the everyday lives of ordinary people. The 1948 fighting over Kashmir apart, this was the first war to be declared against Pakistan after Partition and that, of course, had its own implications.

Qurban, an ageing rickshaw-puller from Anees's hometown of Deoria, and a very dear friend of the family there, decided to come to Delhi to take a stab at a different life, as a cook for my uncle, the legendary history teacher at St. Stephen's College, Mohammad Amin, or Amin sa'ab.

Anees went to receive Qurban from Old Delhi Railway Station and was accompanying him in a tonga at night. Qurban's long beard, coloured in a typical way with khizaab used as a colourant, stereotyped as one used by Muslims, made him stand out at a time when rumours about para-troopers from Pakistan having landed in Delhi were rife. '*Mil gaya, mil gaya!* (We found him, we found him!),' cheered some hotheads on the streets who spotted him and insisted on searching Qurban's luggage for incriminating stuff. After five minutes, Anees suddenly shouted, 'Halt! Do not search that bag, it has explosives.' The enthusiastic search party got excited and dug further, only to find a jar of the famous kartoosi red-chilli pickle from Deoria! They developed some humour at that moment and let Anees and Qurban pass. Anees put it down to not losing his cool.

But such was life, all in a day's work, in 1965. '*Tanaavpurn, lekin niyantran mein*', as the famous line on the state-run All India Radio went: Tense, but under control.

Anees and Sumitra recalled the tension of the time, but it was not explicit and appeared far less threatening than it was to become in later decades. Perhaps the collective memory of having undergone a massive rupture in the form of a break in the name of religion had exhausted some of the hate, they speculated. Nevertheless, no one liked the idea of 'too much independence'. Marriage was considered something beyond the pale. Maybe relationships were okay, but when you married outside lines drawn by caste or region in those times, you crossed boundaries in ways which were not deemed acceptable.

Anees said he and Sumitra never needed to propose. There was no proposal but an unstated understanding firmed up after about six months since they got to know each other, that they would get married.

But the facts remained: Hindu-Muslim, north-south and an 'unusual, reverse' age difference, all stood out like insurmountables. Sumitra chose to not tell her folks, saying that she was alright with informing them rather than trying to seek approval. Her parents dead, and having been brought up by a large-hearted and generous older brother, she did not want to take needless stress in case they erupted.

Anees told his family, and his elder sister reported his intentions to their mother. There was hesitation and a mild degree of unrest in the family. Especially as they lived in a small town, where everyone knew everyone else and it was impossible to hide anything. The Chishti family in Deoria brooded in silence and started to imagine the problems and possible response.

A close friend of my mother's advised her that she must not get angsty about *how* to get married but just do it, and that the nikah ceremony was best, as it did not need a long notice period and could be done quietly. My mother agreed, making things easier for Anees to handle. At least, how the marriage was to take place was decided quickly. They could worry about the names of their children and other such customs later.

Their nikah ceremony, it was decided, would be held at the house of Anees's sister and brother-in-law at St. Stephen's College. Professor Qureshi, the Persian teacher there, volunteered to bring the qazi.

The date for the nikah was set for 12 January 1966, but on the 10th of January, a calamity struck India when Prime Minister Lal Bahadur Shastri died in Tashkent, leaving behind a shell-shocked nation and many unanswered questions. On the day his body came to India, which was a day before the wedding, Anees went to be one with the crowd milling around his house, to feel a oneness with the nation's mood. With a bride set to enter his life the next day, he was experiencing a rush of some very mixed emotions.

The nikah took place the next day in the presence of their close friends and was conducted very quietly. Those in attendance recalled how the bride, confused by the Urdu on the nikahnama, whipped up the floral veil to ask, 'Anees, where do I sign?' This nonchalance and casual enquiry considerably shook the old qazi, but '*qubool hai*' it was.

❧

House-hunting was something Anees and Sumitra recalled partly with nostalgia but also with considerable unease. They were turned back routinely, sometimes upfront and often for things like non-vegetarianism, which was perceived as a problem. It was just shorthand for saying that your surname was not acceptable. Anees had a habit of hanging up an Amrita Sher-Gil painting in the house they would rent, as a ritual. But what he also recalled were the many refusals by landlords, at least three times, when the facts of who he was and that they were born in different faiths proved to be deal-breakers. In one instance, everything was settled, and the Amrita Sher-Gil was hung duly. But having discovered it was not Aneesh but Anees, the landlady begged for them to cancel the lease as 'I didn't realize you were who you are.' Anees recalled pulling down the print of Sher-Gil's famous *Bride's Toilet* from the wall and retorting: 'I too didn't realize who you are. If you think this way, I too don't want to rent your house.'

Legally married, going back to their respective homes in Deoria and Mysore was next on their agenda, a big hurdle to cross, emotionally and functionally.

Deoria

The visit to Deoria was planned for April, which happened to be Bakrid day. The Avadh-Tirhut Mail stopped for only 120 seconds at Deoria Sadar, a blip on the railway map. As Anees stumbled out with his wife and the holdall and case, he was surprised to see a deserted station. It was about five in the evening and the train had arrived late. Soon, however, he was spotted by the biggest liquor trader in the region, Lala Sardari Lal, the leader of the refugees in the town, who shouted, '*Akele aaye ho, bahu kahan hai?* (You've come alone, where's our daughter-in-law?)' Anees greeted that query with some relief and took it as indication that his parents had taken the bull by its horns and informed the town about the events in his life.

Sumitra slowly emerged and met Sardari Lal and they started their journey to their home, a bungalow built by Anees's father. Anees was stunned to find his rather aristocratic father sitting on the steps outside the house, anxious about why his son and his Hindu bride weren't home yet. The delayed train had caused much anxiety and Syed Mohammed Chishti could not bring himself down to relaxing inside.

Meeting the new daughter-in-law was pleasant for Anees's brothers and others in the home and initial hesitation gave way to questions and smiles. Bakrid festivities, in a home with goat sacrifice for each of the three days, meant kilos of meat in the house which Sumitra was keen to see. Her brother-in-law told her that she must not accompany him inside as she was unused to so much meat, but she laughed and said she came from a meat-eating family and was happy to see more of it. The brother-in-law's warnings proved right, though, and Sumitra fainted at the sight of so much goat blood. There was considerable consternation in the usually restrained Chishti household at the implications of the new Hindu bride fainting, but she was made to quickly come around and a good distance between her and the goats was thereon strictly enforced.

A special walima was held the next day where all the eminences in the town came. The Chishtis decided to be completely open and all-embracing about Anees's marital choice. As always was the practice then: people dined together but there was a degree of separation. There were separate cooks for food cooked for Hindus and separate cooks for food for Muslims. Not exactly analogous to vegetarian and non-vegetarian sections today, it was more akin to separateness acknowledged but the right to dine together kept intact. Perhaps more like the Hindus, Parsis and Muslims playing cricket as separate teams at the Bombay Gymkhana?

Girija babu, Anees's old teacher, too turned up to bless their couple. My parents didn't recall any tension and hassle but put that more to graces of the time that prevented an unhinged expression to everything. If there was any resentment or irritation, it was kept under wraps. When my mother went to the market, everyone treated 'Chhoti Dulhan' well, she was shown the finest fabrics by the cloth merchants. There was nothing amiss in the conversations in their shops, courtesies accorded to her as they discussed what would match well with what.

Sumitra, thirty-three years old, did not want to delay having a child, so a daughter was born a year after their wedding. Anees recalled how, after her birth, the question of what she was to be called hung heavy in the air. Anees's mother, on a blue inland, sent an entire list of suggestions: Salma, Niloufer, Zareena, Wahida, Sarah, Marium … with a Seema tucked in somewhere. Sumitra leapt at it. She had volunteered to adopt her husband's surname, happy at the nikah, but for her child, she wanted some ambiguity around how she would be seen. Seema, doubling as both a 'Hindu' and a 'Muslim' name, seemed perfect for Sumitra, and coming from her mother-in-law? It could not be better—bingo. Seema set the limit.

Mysore

Going to Mysore for the first time took some doing for the young couple. There was the guilt of not having told the family there about their nuptials but also, more importantly, the cost of two and a half persons travelling—by the time they gathered the nerve to get there, they had a daughter, who was a little less than three years old.

Anees remembered his brother-in-law, the man who had practically raised Sumitra, vividly. He was among the founders of Kannada cinema, and was making films, including on folklore and Hindu mythology, since the 1940s. He was a freedom fighter and had a breadth of mind that made him a joy to be around. His joie de vivre was the perfect counterfoil to Anees's quietude, and they got on like a house on fire.

Just when he had learned of Sumitra's choice, in 1966, he had written Anees a long letter addressing him as 'Janab' Anees Chishti saheb, perhaps forgetting for a minute that this was no feudal lord but a twenty-six-year-old struggling journalist who was wooing his thirty-three-year-old sister. But Anees understood that Papanna was trying to make a culturally appropriate point, he understood the spirit of the gesture and was very touched.

Sumitra and Seema were already there in Bangalore when Anees arrived. Sumitra, as part of her duties, was to organize a training programme for the Indian Institute of Foreign Trade (IIFT) and after they were done with that, they all drove down to Mysore, on a narrow strip of road they were to take many times from then on.

In Mysore, Anees, a teetotaler and generally restrained person, experienced the warmth of large-hearted and flamboyant hospitality, uniquely reflecting Papanna's world, including his silver screen connections and Mysore, in general.

His nieces, nephews all took to their new uncle with gusto and interest, career advice, a new way of doing this, of somebody who did things differently, whom their beloved and unique aunt was smitten with, and whose presence resulted in giggles and aroused serious interest.

Papanna had a great eye for beautiful shooting locations. Many locales, even today, that Bollywood favours likely bear the imprint of Papanna's keen exploration. His eye for talent also meant he launched new faces who went on to become big stars, including Saroja Devi whom Papanna had discovered and, struck by how she spoke and looked, asked to audition. He had given the Kannada megastar Rajkumar his first role.

The same talent was extended to taking his young brother-in-law to beautiful spots in Karnataka. Two Ambassador cars full of his entire family accompanied them as they set out, whizzing at top speed till both cars were brought to a halt at Srirangapatnam, around noon, all looking expectantly at Anees to get out. He looked quizzically, only to be told that, 'It is Friday, it is already near about one o'clock and this is the mosque Tipu Sultan built. Won't you read the namaz?' Anees found himself in a situation he had never found himself in—hemmed in by two carloads of Hindus, next to a mosque that Tipu built (opposite a temple), insisting that he say his Friday prayers.

Anees Chishti, a leftist by persuasion and then the founder-editor of the Congress (O) paper *Political and Economic Review*, was not amongst those who offered Friday prayers. But overwhelmed by the moment and the gesture, he scrambled out towards the mosque. There, a burly bearded man stopped him from entering. Seeing the young women behind him in colourful sarees, bindis, vermillion and *mallige hoo* (string of jasmine flowers) in their hair as shorthand for a Hindu family out sightseeing, the sidekick of the imam at the mosque thought it fit to bar Anees entry.

Anees eventually had to recite the kalma, like a password and a badge of entry, to persuade the old man to let him enter and read the namaz. The 'Hindus' waited patiently outside Tipu's ruins.

The story of Sumitra and Anees continued to flow, alongside independent India's. The 1970s were an exciting decade.

They would prove to be a shape-shifting decade for India, when recalled with the benefit of hindsight. There was so much that India achieved and lost in that vital decade. So much that was good, as India achieved self-sufficiency in food production, fought a war it won decisively, and buried the two-nation theory for the time being as East Pakistan was transformed into Bangladesh, breaking away from Pakistan. The '70s was the first time that a non-Congress government took charge in India and Indira Gandhi's supremacy was challenged. Apart from fighting a decisive war with Pakistan, India tested nukes, made the first moves to gain self-sufficiency in foodgrains and the Hindi film hero began to be defined as an 'angry young man'.

Later, the 1980s proved unsettling for India and the 1990s even more so. Fissures in India were no longer papered over and the veneer of polite disagreement was slowly giving way to much starker and sharper edges, which were evident in the war cries given during the course of the Rath Yatra of 1990, the subsequent destruction of the Babri Masjid and later when riots broke out in Gujarat in 2002. Repeated electoral victories for the BJP in Gujarat for decades after the 1990s, despite large-scale social mayhem, was telling a story that would only grow louder and more sinister as the twenty-first century rolled out.

Sumitra continued with her intellectual pursuits and her work as an economist at the Indian Institute of Foreign Trade. She served as Director, IIFT, till 1990, before moving to a university campus. She moved to Jawaharlal Nehru University as a professor, fulfilling her own deep desire of spending her sunset years at a university. Sumitra was associated with the Indian School of International Studies, which was based in the red and white sandstone Sapru House in central Delhi, inaugurated by Jawaharlal Nehru in 1955. The school was merged and shifted to JNU in 1969. Having been at Sapru House, going to JNU as a professor had special meaning for her. She authored many books, and her work on transnational corporations, negotiating forums and on developing nations has a salience to this day. Her doctoral thesis on the terms of trade between India and East Europe tells a story of its time beyond just narrow economic concerns.

Anees was the biographer of India's late President Dr Zakir Hussain (1897-1969). As a journalist, he covered the Bhopal Gas Tragedy in 1984. This was a coincidence as he was there as a correspondent for *Eenadu*, covering the general elections. He was practically just swept up in the accident. He wrote a book on the mishap, which is the finest account of a reporter who was among the first to reach the Union Carbide gates, titled *Dateline Bhopal: A Newsman's Diary of the Gas Disaster*. He was a theatre critic for *Shankar's Weekly* and a journalist with *Seminar*, *Economic and Political Weekly* and *Mainstream*. In the early years of *Mainstream,* after this journal was founded in September 1962, he wrote on subjects close to his heart—arts, politics, sports, poetry, languages and science, displaying unusual felicity with a wide range of subjects. As mentioned before, Sumitra ghostwrote for the same magazine and some very considerable portions when Nikhil Chakravarty was the editor. Her writings on economics tackled big issues of inequity and the absence of fair rules guiding trade between large and smaller countries, still dealing with the aftermath of centuries-long colonial subjugation. For some time, Anees functioned as this periodical's assistant editor.

In an essay on the completion of five decades of *Mainstream*, Anees wrote: 'Fifty years! Looking back, it does not seem to be too long a period: perhaps only yesterday, or a week or fortnight ago. Spending long Tuesday night hours, correcting galley proofs, sitting in a small room at Kesar Kiari Printing Press near Bara Hindu Rao surrounded by racks loaded with tons of lead in the form of typefaces to be used for hand composing of pages of *Mainstream* to be ready for printing by the morning. Small delights like savouring delicious mutton curry and tandoori rotis from a dhaba, in good company, at times with the loved one who was later to become the life-partner. Thanks, *Mainstream*, for these delights! Looking at *Mainstream*, displayed in the best known news-stands from Thiruvanthapuram and Bangalore to Delhi, from Kolkata to Mumbai, all those fifty years seem to be a dream, a delightful dream, indeed!'

Subsequently, they both co-edited *Alpjan*, a forum for voices of people that went unrepresented, voices of various types of minorities. He was keen to see it go online but that did not eventually take place in his lifetime. It has a digital presence now.

Whether it was the Emergency or the tremors of the demolition of the Babri Masjid that changed India, Anees and Sumitra realized slowly that the hurdles they thought they had faced when they got together were simply genteel objections compared to what the country was now experiencing.

In all this—*Mainstream*, terms of trade, fierce and enriching debates and bi-annual trips home, alternating between Deoria and Mysore—it slowly emerged that in the Chishti household, it was the kitchen that had unknowingly become the keeper of the composite secrets and essence of India.

Sumitra, from a radically different culinary tradition, and a 'working' woman at that, was deeply interested in matters of the gut and stomach and, along with Anees and his family's support, ran a most interesting kitchen.

In a small and middle-class space, nothing fancy or particularly Nawabi or Rajwada about it, the two went on to run one of the most delicious and wholesome spaces for a kitchen of India. The approaches to food spoke of the eclectic and easy togetherness that has later been unfairly read down as merely tolerance. It was different and much more than sufferance. Food, like shared lives, made new dishes, aromas and sights possible. In older times, kitchens were segregated spaces. But not Anees and Sumitra's. Taboos were taboo. It was beyond live and let live. It was a confluence and khichdi—which, it would not be far-fetched to say, was a symbol of a unique civilizational moment in South Asia which made India the exemplar or the exception, an island then amongst the divisive ethnic nationalisms that ensured sharedness did not exist or, where it managed to exist, could not flourish.

My mother went on to compile a recipe book for me, of delectable yet simple recipes of both Karnataka and Uttar Pradesh, both 'Hindu' and 'Muslim', Kshatriya and Syed, vegetarian and non-vegetarian.

These dishes evoke the taste of a khichdi home that confidently experimented, borrowed, shared and ended up brewing a very special dish. It is called India.

Recipes

My parents were both first-generation migrants to Delhi representing a very important slice of Indian urban life as they set up home in the late 1960s. Sumitra, a working mother, like many of her time, did find herself being in-charge of the kitchen, spending time there, growing a few herbs and ingredients in pots, the curry leaf and mint. Ingredients, too, were different then—the whole turmeric as a root was used more as there was no turmeric powder easily available, coconut milk had to be pressed and extracted from fresh coconuts, and the texture of the the masala, hand-ground, was different from what the blender yielded. Pre-mixed batter for idli/dosa was unthinkable and being mindful of fermentation time was routine.

It is not without reason that a very important part of Anees, Sumitra and India's story is told through the food they ate and fed those around them. Home-made meals were when friends and family came together and looked in wonder at the mishmash of north and south, the 'Hindu' and the 'Muslim', as a bit of India was always brewing in their small home.

That is why, this recipe book is an important facet of their story and embodies the Ganga-Jamuni or the tale of confluence that marked the old India, which is fast being demonized today.

More generally speaking, food history is serious history and sometimes the best way to tell a larger story.

Like the ingredients that make it, food crossed cultural boundaries centuries before the word 'globalization' entered our lexicon. Take the example of the samosa. One account of its origin traces it to Central Asia. The crisp triangular patty did not come to India with conquerors, but traders. According to the leading food historian K.T. Achaya, in about 1300 CE, the poet Amir Khusrau, describing the food of the Muslim aristocracy in Delhi, wrote of 'the samosa prepared from meat, ghee and onion'. About fifty years later, according to Achaya, the famous scholar and explorer Ibn Battuta calls it samusak, describing it as 'minced meat cooked with almonds, walnuts, pistachios, onions and spices placed inside a thin envelope of wheat and deep fried in ghee'. Over the passage of time, the snack adapted to vegetarian tastes in the subcontinent.

Culinary histories often used the term 'indigenization' to describe the samosa's journey in its adopted land. But the word reveals less than it hides. Potato, the pièce de résistance of the Indian samosa, finds mention in food histories of the subcontinent only in the late seventeenth century. Similarly, chaat, another much-loved snack of the country, also traces its origin to the Mughal courts in the seventeenth century. It acquired its favourite ingredient much later.

Like several cultural artefacts, the food that we eat is a potpourri of influences. Of course, like histories of the origins of communities or social groups, narratives about the origins of food have contested versions.

In the same way that who one marries or talks to or where one lives could be a criminal act (because of new laws on so-called 'forced conversions' and restrictions on renting homes to certain communities), food has also become a bitterly contested terrain. What one eats or does not eat is picked at as a differentiator. That is at the heart of new laws around cattle, beef consumption, halal food or mid-day meals too, where politics decides whether eggs will be served to malnourished children.

What this politics of food has tried to erase is a consciousness and knowledge of common roots, exchange of ideas and cross-fertilization that made modern food choices possible. Travellers from distant lands brought new ingredients, seeds, vegetables and fruits. These enabled new ways of eating and cooking, with constant borrowing and lending of dishes, ways of cooking, spices or marinating foods nourishing the process. The samosa may not be as home-grown as we like to believe, or the tandoori chicken for that matter. At the same time, things targeted for being 'foreign'—like Mughlai cuisine sometimes is—are indigenous, having travelled in another form and then having been perfected in the shape and taste we know today, right here—in India, in Mughal times. Both of these are as Indian as they can be.

Food, if anything, must remind us of how much we reside in the world outside and how much of the world outside resides in us. Deep, inside our gut.

The Recipe Book

I have often attempted to write a book on Indian cooking. It is indeed a tall claim for, in my opinion, it is extremely difficult if not impossible to consolidate all the recipes of the varied food available in India. Very few countries in the world offer a connoisseur of food such a wide variety, of vegetarian and non-vegetarian foods, as we have in India. So, I do not pretend to cover this magnificent variety our nation offers. Rather, this is a very small attempt to record some variety that I know and have cooked satisfactorily.

Writing a cookery book is more difficult than I had anticipated. I have written a number of books on technical subjects—on economics and international relations. I began with an unwarranted confidence to write this book as well. The moment I began this exercise I realized what I am getting into. Yet I persisted in the effort.

The inspiration for this came from my daughter. Like many young women of the modern generation, she does not enjoy cooking. So I thought that I should leave a book of recipes for her, which she can consult when she wants to eat any specific dish that she had enjoyed in her mother's cooking.

This is my third attempt, and the last one.

I only hope that readers will find it useful to try some of the recipes given in this book. Good luck to those who eat the food cooked from these recipes!

Prof. Sumitra Chishti
2001

Rice

Since rice is a primary diet in a number of states in India, I will begin by giving some recipes of the varied ways of cooking rice.

(a) Plain rice (with starch)

Plain rice is the simplest dish to cook.

Ingredients

250 gm white rice
500 gm water

Preparation

Wash the rice and clear the water. Then add the 500 gm water. Place it on the stove. Stir it when it boils. After two-thirds of the cooking is done, put the flame on simmer. Leave it for 5-8 minutes. The rice is cooked. It is very good to serve it hot. If it is warmed in a microwave, with a few sprinklings of water, you may regain the original flavour.

(b) Rice without starch

Preparation

Follow the method above. But do not leave the rice to cook fully. In the middle, strain the water from rice and stir well, leave it on sim flame for 5-8 minutes. Remove it from the stove, serve hot.

Zeera rice

Ingredients

250 gm of rice
500 gm of water
2 tsp cumin seeds
2 tbsp cooking oil
Salt to taste

Preparation

Wash the rice and keep it separately. Take a vessel, add cooking oil. After it is heated, put cumin seeds. When the seeds turn brown, put rice, mix cumin seeds and rice well, put salt and add water to it.

Cook the rice the same way as plain rice. Serve hot. It is good to eat this rice with either vegetarian, chicken or mutton curry.

Biryani (mutton)*

Ingredients

250 gm rice
500 gm mutton
5 pieces of cloves/1 tbsp of dry coriander seeds
4 small pieces of cinnamon
10 garlic cloves
4 small green cardamoms
3 big black cardamoms
A small piece of ginger
4 tbsp of cooking oil
One large onion, chopped
Salt to taste

Preparation

Wash the mutton, add four cups of water, add salt, mix half the cloves, cardamoms, garlic and ginger.

Put the dry coriander seeds and chopped ginger in a clean muslin cloth and place it with the mutton. Boil it in a pressure cooker for 15-20 minutes.

---

* Same method can be used for chicken biryani too.

Take the cooked mutton and remove the coriander and ginger by squeezing their juice into the mutton and keep it separately.

Separate this soup from the mutton.

Take the rice and wash it, keep it aside. Take a vessel, put the cooking oil and turn on the heat. Put cardamoms, remaining cloves, bay leaves, chopped onions and fry. Add the mutton and gently stir for 2-3 minutes, then add the washed rice and mix it and stir for 3-4 minutes. Add the soup and water to the rice. Add necessary salt. Stir well, and cook the rice for 10 minutes. Leave it on simmer.

Remove it when it is finally cooked.

You may add some cooking colour over the rice.

Rice with vegetables cooked in coconut milk

Ingredients

250 gm rice
100 gm beans
100 gm cauliflower
50 gm carrots
100 gm peas
4 green chillies
One pod of garlic (make a paste)
1 fresh coconut
2 tbsp of oil
Salt to taste

Preparation

Cut and clean the vegetables.

Grate the coconut and take out its milk. (Put the grated coconut in a grinder. Grind it for few minutes. Remove it and squeeze it to take milk. You may use a strainer/sieve for this.)

Make a paste with the garlic. In a vessel, heat oil and add the paste and green chillies. Add all the chopped vegetables and salt. Leave it for 10 minutes on sim flame. Once the vegetables are semi-cooked, add rice and stir. Add coconut milk and water accordingly. Take water and mix it with coconut milk, approximately two big glasses, and add salt.

Leave it on sim for 10 minutes, until the rice gets cooked.

Tahadi-rice with vegetables

Ingredients

250 gm rice
100 gm beans
100 gm cauliflower
50 gm carrots
100 gm peas
3 medium-sized tomatoes
3-4 bay leaves
2 cloves
2 small pieces of cinnamon
1 tbsp coriander power
1 tsp turmeric powder
1 tsp red chilli powder
2 medium-sized onions
½ pod of garlic
1 medium-sized piece of ginger
2 tbsp cooking oil
Salt to taste

Preparation

Cut all the vegetables, keep cut tomatoes separately. Also cut the onions, peel the garlic and grate the ginger. Make a paste of coriander power, chilli powder, turmeric power, garlic, ginger and the cut onions.

Pour cooking oil in a vessel and heat it. Put cloves and cinnamon and also the other cut onions and fry. After the onions turn brown, add the ground masala, salt and tomato. Stir it for a while, put all the vegetables and add half a cup of water. Put it on sim flame for 6-8 minutes.

Take the rice and wash it. Add the washed rice in the vegetables and stir it. Pour two big glasses of water and mix well. Allow the rice and vegetables to cook (after adding a little more salt, if you wish) over medium flame. When the water has almost evaporated, leave the cooked rice and vegetables on sim flame for 10 minutes. Remove it and serve with any chutney.

Mutton dishes

Mutton korma*

Ingredients

250 gm mutton
2 tbsp poppy seeds
1 tbsp coriander powder
½ pod garlic
1 medium-sized red chilli
2 cloves
2 small pieces of cinnamon sticks
3 medium-sized onions
1 tbsp curd
Salt to taste

Preparation

Cut onions, grate ginger and cut garlic.

Divide the cut onions into two parts. Poppy seeds to be roasted moderately on the tawa, taking care not to burn

---

* Chicken can also be cooked in the same manner. No need to use the pressure cooker. Chicken tastes far better if the pressure cooker is not used.

it. Make a powder of poppy seeds, cloves and cinnamon in the grinder.

Take coriander powder, garlic, chillies, ginger, and onions and make a paste of it along with the poppy seed powder with cloves and cinnamon that you have made. Take the vessel, put oil and heat it. Put 1/3 of cut onions and fry. Add the masala to the onions, and then add the washed mutton and salt to taste. Fry it for 10-15 minutes and add the curd. Add enough water to cook. Cook in a pressure cooker for 15 minutes. See to it that the gravy is not watery and the mutton is cooked and tender. Cut green coriander leaves and sprinkle them on the curry.

Mutton curry

Ingredients

250 gm mutton
3 medium-sized onions
2 medium-sized tomatoes
2 cloves
2 cinnamon sticks (small)
1 tbsp coriander powder
½ pod of garlic
1 medium-sized piece of ginger
1 tsp turmeric powder
½ tsp red chilli powder
1 tbsp cooking oil
Salt to taste

Preparation

Wash the mutton and cut 2 of the 3 onions into small pieces. Peel the garlic and cut the ginger into fine pieces or grate it, also chop the tomatoes. Take coriander powder, garlic, cloves, cinnamon sticks, ginger, turmeric powder and cut onions and make a paste. Heat 1 tbsp oil in a pressure cooker and add the 2/3 cut onions. Fry them until brown. Put in the masala along with cut tomatoes.

Add the washed mutton and salt after five minutes. Fry it nicely till the masala gets cooked. Add water so that mutton gets cooked and a nice thick gravy is ready. Leave the pressure cooker on for 15 minutes. Open it once done and sprinkle coriander leaves on it.

Mutton do pyaza*

Ingredients

250 gm mutton
500 gm onions
3 cloves
3 small pieces of cinnamon sticks
2 red chillies,
3-4 bay leaves
1 tbsp curd
2 cardamoms
1 pod of garlic
1 small medium-sized piece of ginger
1 tbsp cooking oil
Salt to taste

Preparation

Cut the onions into small pieces. Grate the garlic and ginger. Wash the mutton.

---

* Chicken do pyaza can also be cooked in the same way and with the same masala.

Take the pressure cooker, pour oil in it and heat it. Put the cardamoms, cloves, cinnamon sticks and bay leaves in. Add onions and fry them until brown.

Add the mutton, salt and fry it all well. Then add the curd and continue to fry.

Add one and a half glasses of water and let the pressure cooker sit for 15 minutes.

When you open the pressure cooker, check how much water is left. Make sure the mutton is semi-dry, if not drier.

Keema matar/aloo/ beans

(Mutton keema)*

Ingredients

250 gm keema

1 tbsp coriander powder

1 tsp turmeric powder

1 tsp chilli powder

4 cloves

2 pieces of cinnamon

2 tomatoes

2 onions

6 cloves of garlic

1 medium-sized piece of ginger

150 gm peas/two potatoes cut into small pieces/50 gm green beans

Fresh coriander leaves

3 tbsp curd

Salt to taste

---

* Chicken keema can also be cooked in the same manner and does not need a pressure cooker. It is better to cook without a pressure cooker.

Preparation

Cut the onions. Make a paste with one onion and all the other masalas. (Use a pressure cooker, if you prefer).

Pour the cooking oil. Put in the cut onions, fry them till they are brown, add the paste and two cut tomatoes. Fry the masala along with the keema and add water. If you want dry keema, add only two cups of water along with the vegetable of your choice.

Take out the meat and add salt and the vegetables in the pressure cooker. Cook for 5 minutes. Add some onions and fry them till brown, then add the keema, and fry well. Add a little curd and fry more. Then, after adding some water, close the pressure cooker and let it cook for 15 minutes. If there is water left after you open it, leave it on the stove till the keema is semi dry. Sprinkle coriander leaves on top as dressing.

Keema and green methi (fenugreek)

Same as the other keema preparation, except you put in green methi in this. The methi must not be too much in quantity. Similarly, you can put in palak with keema.

Mutton pasanda

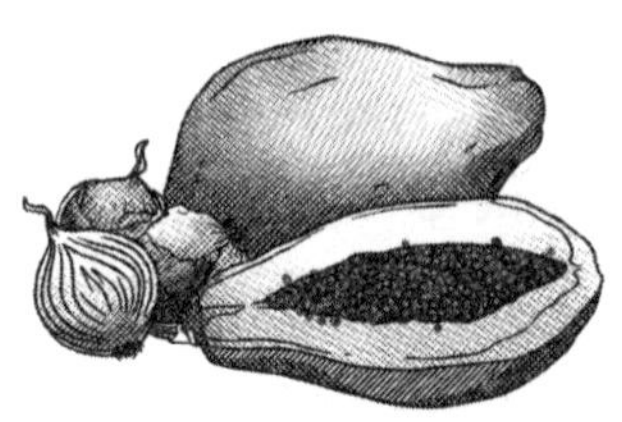

(Pasanda requires asking the butcher to give you boneless, flattened, battered meat pieces. Most butchers will be able to do it for you. In this dish, the art lies in the preparation of the mutton.)

Ingredients

500 gm mutton cut into pasanda pieces (flat and battered)
½ small green (raw) papaya
1½ tbsp of cooking oil
4 cloves
4 small cinnamon sticks
2 large onions
1 pod of garlic
1 medium-sized ginger
½ tbsp poppy seeds
2 tbsp curd
Salt to taste

Preparation

Cut onions into small pieces and divide into two equal halves. Grate the garlic, ginger and papaya. Roast the poppy seeds on a tawa for 3-4 minutes and make a dry powder of it, set it aside. Take half of the onions and the other masala items, including papaya, and make a paste. Wash the mutton. Mix the masala paste, salt and curd and leave it to marinate for 6 hours.

Take the pressure cooker, add oil and heat it. Put the remaining onions in and fry nicely. Add the marinated mutton along with ground poppy seeds and fry for 10 minutes. (If necessary, cook the mutton in the pressure cooker for 10 minutes). Open the lid of the pressure cooker and continue to cook and dry the mutton. After it dries, put in green coriander leaves.

I recommend roasting cumin seeds by frying on a tawa and then making a dry powder out of it. Sprinkle it on the pasanda while serving.

Mutton korma (Karnataka style)*

Ingredients

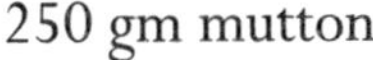

250 gm mutton
2 medium-sized tomatoes
2 medium-sized onions
½ pod of garlic
1 medium-sized ginger
1 tsp sambhar powder
1 tbsp cooking oil (777 brown is good)
1 green chilli
1 tbsp coriander powder
½ fresh coconut (or even ¼ dry coconut)
1 tsp turmeric powder
2 cloves
2 pieces of cinnamon sticks
Salt to taste

Preparation

Cut onions into pieces, grate ginger, cut tomatoes into pieces and add green chillies. Peel and grate the garlic.

---

* Chicken can also be cooked in the same manner.

Make a paste of coriander powder, 1 cut onion, sambhar powder, turmeric, cloves, garlic and ginger. Make a paste of the grated coconut separately.

Heat oil in a pressure cooker. Add the remaining onion and make it brown, put the masala paste along with the washed mutton and cut tomatoes, fry it and add salt. Pour 4 cups of water and close the pressure cooker.

Cook the mutton for 15 minutes, then open the pressure cooker and add the coconut paste. Boil it for 3-4 minutes. Sprinkle green coriander leaves before serving.

Serve hot.

Note: You may cook green methi with the same masala. Take 200 gm green methi (just the plucked leaves) and put it in along with the mutton. You may also add potatoes, if you wish to.

Fried mutton (Karnataka style)

Ingredients

250 gm mutton
2 medium-sized onions
1 green chilli
1 tsp sambhar powder
½ tbsp coriander powder
1 tsp turmeric powder
½ pod of garlic
1 small-sized ginger piece
2 cloves
2 small pieces of cinnamon sticks
¼ dry/fresh coconut
1 tbsp cooking oil
Salt to taste

Preparation

Chop the onions. Along with peeled and grated garlic and ginger respectively, add half of the chopped onions and make a paste. Then grate the coconut. Mix all these things into one paste.

Heat oil in a pressure cooker and add the remaining chopped onions. Make them brown. Add the cloves and cinnamon. Then add the mutton and the paste. Add 2-3 cups of water and salt. Close the pressure cooker. Cook it for 15 minutes. After opening the pressure cooker, fry the mutton until the water has dried.

Sprinkle green coriander leaves on it while serving.

This tastes well with rice and sambhar.

Shami kabab

Ingredients

250 gm mutton keema
1 medium-sized onion
½ pod of garlic
1 raw egg
1 medium-sized ginger
2 cloves
2 medium-sized cinnamon sticks
2 red chillies
½ cup chana dal
Oil as required
Fresh mint and coriander leaves
Salt to taste

Preparation

Cut the onions, grate the ginger and peel and chop the garlic. Add 2 cups of water to the masala and boil it along with the chana dal and keema, preferably not in a pressure cooker. Boil until cooked. Allow the water to dry completely. Make a paste in the grinder, without adding any extra water.

Take egg whites, beat it and mix it with the keema paste. Add mint/green coriander leaves. Divide the keema into small portions, make small round balls of it and then flatten them. Take a non-stick frying pan, pour 1 tbsp oil and heat it. Shallow fry 2-3 kababs at one go; fry them on both sides.

Repeat the operation. Serve with thinly sliced round onions.

Mutton kofta (Karnataka style)*

Ingredients

250 gm keema
½ fresh/dry coconut
½ cup gram powder
1 green chilli
1 tsp sambhar powder
½ tbsp coriander powder
2 cloves
2 medium-sized cinnamon sticks
2 medium-sized onions
½ pod of garlic
1 medium-sized ginger piece
1 tsp turmeric
Salt to taste
2 tbsp of curd
1 tbsp of cooking oil

* Chicken mince meatballs can also be prepared in the same manner.

Preparation

Grate the coconut and chop the onions. Divide it into two equal parts.

Peel and chop the garlic and grate the ginger. Mix all this with cloves, cinnamon, coriander powder, chopped green chillies, turmeric and make a paste.

Divide the paste into two equal parts.

Take a small kadhai (deep frying pan) and heat it.

Fry the remaining onions until they are brown. Add one portion of masala along with the curd, add salt and fry it for five minutes over the medium flame.

Take the other half of the masala and mix it with the keema. Add some salt and gram powder, mix well and make keema balls.

Put these balls into the masala and add water carefully, and stir it.

After one boil, put this mixture on slow flame and let it simmer for 10-12 minutes.

Sprinkle green coriander leaves while serving. Serve hot.

Chicken fry (simple)

Ingredients

6 legs/breasts of chicken
2 red chillies
4 cloves
3 cinnamon sticks
1 pod of garlic
1 big piece of ginger
2 tbsp cooking oil
Salt to taste

Preparation

Make a paste of the red chillies, cloves, cinnamon, garlic and ginger.

Wash the chicken legs/breast and marinate these with the masala for 3-4 hours.

Take the frying pan, heat the oil and fry these over the fires till they become tender as well as red.

Chicken fry with masala

Ingredients

6 leg pieces/breast pieces of chicken

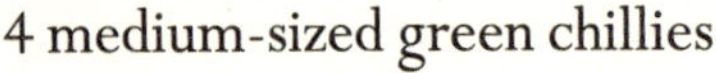

4 medium-sized green chillies

1 big piece of ginger

1 pod of garlic

6 tbsp curd

6 cloves

6 small pieces of cinnamon sticks

2 tbsp refined flour (maida)

Salt to taste

2 tbsp cooking oil

Preparation

Make a paste of the ginger, garlic, chillies, cloves and cinnamon. Marinate the chicken with the masala and curd for 6-8 hours. Add water to the maida and make a thin paste with some salt. Cover each piece of the marinated chicken with the paste of maida. Take the frying pan and pour the required amount of oil for deep frying. Put in the pieces of chicken in and fry them till they are deep brown.

Chicken roast

Ingredients

½ kg chicken
2 red chillies
2 cloves
2 cinnamon pieces
2 large onions
½ pod of garlic
1 medium-sized piece of ginger

Preparation

Cut the onions (divide them into two parts, one for the paste and the other for chopping and frying). Peel and chop the garlic and grate the ginger, make a paste of all with one half of the chopped onions.

Take a cooking vessel and pour oil in it. After heating the oil add the rest of the onions and fry until they are brown. Add the chicken and the paste along with salt and some water.

Cook the chicken till it is tender.

Stir well till it is cooked and the water has dried.

If you like, you can squeeze some lemon juice on it. You may also put some curd in the last stages of cooking, if you wish to.

Mutton chops

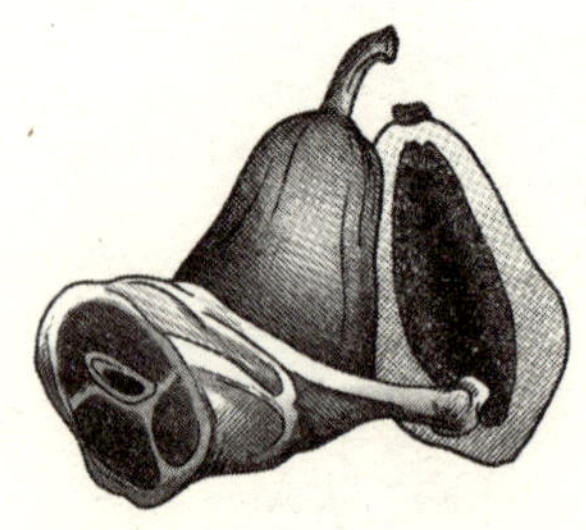

Ingredients

10 mutton chops
4-5 tbsp cooking oil
2 pods of garlic
1 medium-sized ginger
2 red chillies
1 large onion
1 small piece of tender green papaya
4 tbsp curd
Salt to taste

Preparation

Make a paste of all the ingredients, except the mutton and the curd.

Wash the mutton chops, add the paste, salt, curd and marinate for at least two hours.

Pour oil in a frying pan, heat it, put in the marinated chops; shallow fry on a slow flame for 20-30 minutes. Serve hot.

Chicken with coconut milk

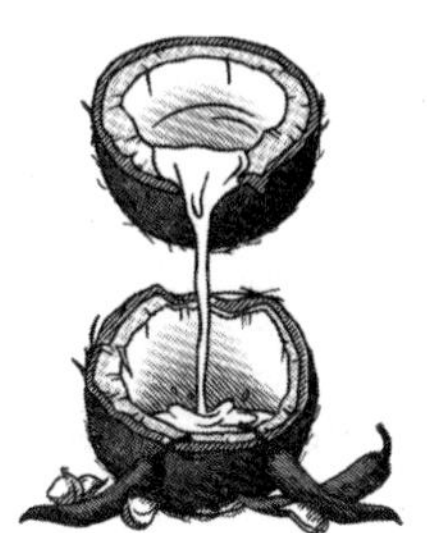

Ingredients

½ kg chicken
1 fresh coconut or coconut milk
2 green chillies
1 pod of garlic
Salt to taste

Preparation

If readymade coconut milk is not available, extract milk from grated coconut by pressing it. Put the chicken and milk together along with the garlic, chillies and salt in a vessel and cook until it is tender. See to it that too much water is not added, but just enough to make the curry. Serve it with rice.

Chicken chops

Ingredients

6 chicken chops
1 pod garlic
2 cinnamon sticks
4 cloves of garlic
2 tbsp oil
1 medium-sized ginger
4 tbsp curd
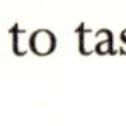
Salt to taste

Preparation

Marinate the chicken with curd and salt.

Make a paste of the garlic, ginger, cloves and cinnamon. Add this to the marinated chicken chops, leave them for an hour and a half (an hour is reasonable time).

Take a frying pan. Pour two tablespoons of oil and heat it. Drop in the chicken chops and fry them on low flame until it gets cooked.

Simple roast chicken (marinated)

Ingredients

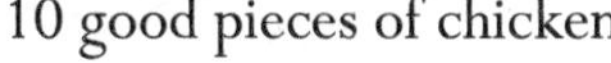

10 good pieces of chicken
4 cloves
4 cinnamon sticks
1 pod of garlic
1 onion
1 small piece of ginger
2 tbsp curd
1 tbsp cooking oil
Salt to taste

Preparation

Marinate the chicken with salt and curd for an hour.

Chop the onions and garlic and grate the ginger. Make a paste of the garlic, ginger, cloves and cinnamon.

Take a small kadhai. Heat the oil and fry the chopped onion in until brown, add the paste and the marinated chicken. Stir well.

Add a cup of water, leave it on a low flame for 25 minutes. Stir it often till it is cooked. There should be a little sauce or gravy.

Dals

Arhar ki dal

Ingredients

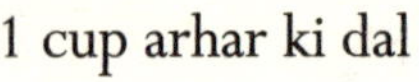

1 cup arhar ki dal
1 tsp turmeric powder
1 tsp salt
1 tsp chilli powder
5 cups of water
1 tsp cumin seeds
5-6 cloves of garlic
½ tbsp of oil

Preparation

Add the washed dal and other ingredients (except cumin seeds and garlic) in a pressure cooker.

Boil for 3-4 minutes. Stir well after you open the lid.

Take the oil in a kadhai, heat it, drop the cumin seeds and garlic. Fry until they turn brown and smell good. Add this to the dal.

Sambhar

Ingredients

1 cup arhar ki dal

1 tbsp sambhar powder (777, preferably)

1 tsp turmeric powder

10 curry leaves

250-350 gm vegetables (preferred vegetables are: cauliflower, green beans, potatoes; you can also add ladyfinger, but after chopping and frying them)

5-8 grams of tamarind

½ tsp rye seeds

6-7 garlic cloves

Salt to taste

Preparation

Boil dal with all the ingredients, except tamarind, for a period of 5 minutes in the pressure cooker.

Soak the tamarind in a cup of water for 10 minutes. Squeeze the tamarind and strain the water.

When the dal and vegetables are cooked, add the strained tamarind water. Boil it nicely. Don't close the pressure cooker.

After 5-8 minutes, turn off the stove.

Pop the rye/mustard seeds along with a few chopped pieces of garlic as the tadka.

Add this to the dal and the sambhar is ready.

Chana (chickpeas)*

Ingredients

125 gm kabuli chana (soaked in water for 4-5 hours)

4 tomatoes

1 tbsp coriander powder

1 tsp chilli powder

1 tsp turmeric powder

2 large onions

1 pod of garlic

1 piece of ginger

1 sprout of mint and some coriander leaves

2 tbsp of oil

Preparation

Put the washed chana into a pressure cooker with salt and water.

Make a paste of coriander, garlic, ginger, chilli powder, turmeric powder and one chopped onion.

---

* You can prepare rajma (kidney beans) in the same manner.

Pour the oil in the same pressure cooker and heat it (after removing chana and keeping it in another vessel). Put the other chopped onion in the hot oil and fry until it turns brown, then add the masala along with a little salt and chopped tomatoes.

Fry the masala for a while and put the boiled chana in it along with the water.

Let it mix nicely and boil for 10 minutes. Sprinkle coriander and mint leaves on top and serve hot.

Dal-palak

Ingredients

1 cup arhar ki dal
300 gm palak
1 tsp red chilli powder
1 tsp turmeric powder
2 tsp cumin seeds
2 tsp oil

Preparation

Chop well-washed palak into small pieces and wash again.

Add the palak and the washed dal in water and put all the ingredients, except cumin seeds, in a pressure cooker and cook for 6-7 minutes.

Remove the vessel from the stove.

Stir well. Put tadka with cumin seeds.

Rasams

Mysore rasam

Ingredients

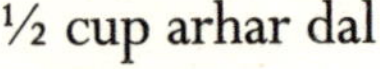

½ cup arhar dal

4 tomatoes

1 tbsp sambhar/rasam powder (777, preferably)

1 tsp turmeric powder

5-10 gm tamarind

Coriander leaves, mustard seeds, rye seeds and curry leaves

Salt to taste

Preparation

Boil the washed dal with tomatoes, turmeric powder and salt for five minutes.

Remove it from the stove. After it cools a little, strain it in a strainer. Smash the dal and tomato left in the strainer well and add this and a cup of water back into the strained dal water.

Also add the soaked and strained tamarind water along with sambhar powder.

Boil it well with curry leaves. See to it that the rasam does not become thick but remains liquid.

Pop rye and mustard seeds as a tadka on top and the Mysore rasam is ready.

Rasam

Ingredients

1.5 litre water
3 tomatoes
2 tsp cumin seeds
1 and ½ tsp of black pepper
1 pod of garlic
2 red chillies
1 tsp mustard seeds
1 and ½ tbsp tamarind
Curry leaves and fresh coriander
Salt to taste

Preparation

Put the soaked and strained tamarind water into the bowl of water, add salt and chopped tomatoes too.

Make a paste of garlic, cumin and pepper.

Put that into the water along with other ingredients.

Heat the oil, put mustard seeds, chillies and curry leaves.

After it is done, add this into the mixture of water and boil some more.

Sprinkle chopped fresh coriander leaves on top and serve.

Rasam

Ingredients

½ cup of arhar dal
salt to taste
1 tbsp turmeric
1 tbsp tamarind
½ pod of garlic
1 tsp mustard seeds
1 tbsp sambhar powder
2 tomatoes
(More mustard seeds and curry leaves for additional tadka, if desired)

Preparation

Boil the dal with salt and turmeric.

Take the cooking vessel, heat the oil in it, add mustard seeds and chopped garlic.

Then add the boiled dal, chopped tomatoes, soaked and strained tamarind water, and sambhar powder. Boil it all well.

If you want, give tadka once again by repeating the popping of mustard seeds and some curry leaves on top.

Kadhi

Ingredients

A bowl of slightly sour curd

2-3 tbsp of besan (chickpea flour)

1 medium-sized bottle gourd (lauki)

1 onion

1 pod of garlic

1 tsp turmeric powder

1 medium-sized piece of ginger

1 tbsp oil

1 and ½ tsp methi

1 and ½ tsp chilli powder

2 red chillies

Cumin seeds

Salt to taste

Preparation

Mix curd and chickpea flour well with turmeric and keep it aside.

Chop the onions and garlic and grate the ginger. Make a paste of it along with chillies or chilli powder.

Peel lauki, cut it into medium-sized pieces. Boil it separately with salt. Add the boiled pieces into the curd mixture. Take a vessel; heat the oil, add the methi.

After methi turns brown, add the paste and after 2-3 minutes add the lauki.

See to it that the mixture is not too thick. Add some water, if needed.

Boil it for 5-8 minutes, give a tadka of cumin seeds.

Kadhi with pakodas

The ingredients and preparation for this are the same as for kadhi earlier, except lauki is not to be added and pakodas need to be prepared.

Preparation

Take half a cup of besan, put salt, half a teaspoon of chilli powder, half a teaspoon of turmeric powder.

Mix it well; it should be of a consistency to form small balls. Fry them lightly in oil.

Along with this, heat water in a small vessel.

Put the fried pakoras in hot water and then after taking them out with a deep spoon minus the excess water, add them into the kadhi mixture.

Baingan ka bharta

Ingredients

2 round, medium-sized brinjals
2 large onions
3-4 pieces of green chillies
1 medium-sized garlic
3-4 tomatoes
2 tbsp oil
Salt to taste

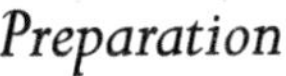

Preparation

Take the baingan and roast it directly on the stove.

Chop onions, tomatoes, chillies and ginger. Smash in the roasted baingan.

Take a kadhai. Pour some oil in it and heat it. Add the chopped onions and medium-fry them, then add in the baingan, tomatoes, ginger and green chillies with salt.

Stir well for 10-15 minutes.

Sprinkle coriander leaves as garnish.

Aloo ka bharta

Ingredients

4-5 medium-sized potatoes
2 onions
2 tbsp salt to taste
3-4 cinnamon pieces

Preparation

Boil the potatoes well. Peel them and smash them well. Put oil in a kadhai. Put in the chopped onions and fry them, then add the mashed potatoes and salt and stir well.

Make a powder of the cinnamon, and sprinkle the powder on the cooked potato 'paste' in the kadhai.

Paneer ki sabzi

Ingredients

200 gm paneer
2 large onions
2 green chillies
2 large tomatoes
1 tbsp cooking oil
Coriander leaves
Salt to taste

Preparation

Grate the paneer and chop the tomatoes and green chillies into small pieces. Chop onion.

Pour oil in a small kadhai and heat it. Add the chopped onions, fry them until they are light brown. Add the chopped tomatoes and stir. Put in the grated paneer along with salt and stir well.

Let it all cook for 5 minutes and keep on stirring. Sprinkle chopped coriander leaves on top and serve.

Paneer fry

Ingredients

Paneer 200 gm
Cumin seeds powder (roasted)
2 tbsp cooking oil
Salt to taste

Preparation

Cut paneer into small cubes.

Take a frying pan, put the oil and heat it. Fry the paneer cubes on slow flame. Add salt and the cumin seed powder.

Paneer curry

Ingredients

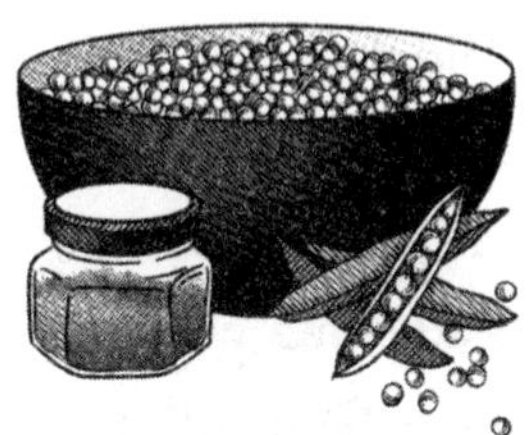

200 gm paneer
2 tomatoes
100 gm peas
1 tbsp coriander powder
1 tsp turmeric powder
1 tsp chilli powder
2 onions
½ pod of garlic
1 small-sized ginger
Fresh coriander leaves
2 tbsp cooking oil
Salt to taste

Preparation

Cut the paneer into medium-sized cubes. If you want, fry the pieces, though they taste very good even without frying.

Make a paste of all the powders, one chopped onion, garlic and ginger.

Then chop the other onion and cut the tomatoes into small pieces.

Take a kadhai and heat some oil in it.

Add the cut onions and fry till they are brown.

Add the paste, salt and cut tomatoes. Pour some water and stir it well.

Fry the masala well till the raw smell disappears.

Add some water, stir well and add the peas, leaving it on a low flame till the peas are cooked and the gravy turns thick.

Add the paneer and stir again, let it settle for a bit.

Then add fresh coriander leaves as dressing.

Fish curry

Ingredients

½ kg fish (Rohu or Surmai)
1 tbsp coriander powder
1 tsp chilli powder
1 tsp turmeric powder
2 onions
4 cloves
3-4 pieces of cinnamon sticks
1 pod of garlic
1 medium-sized ginger
1 and ½ spoonful of methi
2 tbsp cooking oil, preferably mustard oil
2 tbsp of curd
Salt to taste

Preparation

Wash the fish with turmeric (it takes away the smell).

Make a paste of all the spices, except methi.

Heat the oil, pop methi seeds and when they turn brown, add the spice paste. Fry the masala well after adding the curd.

After it is well done, add the fish and stir well, but be careful to not break the pieces. Add some water, but not too much, just enough to cover the fish. Fish does not take much time to cook. Keep on stirring and checking whether the fish is cooked. Once the fish is done, remove the pan from the stove, and let it settle for a few minutes before serving.

Smashed fish

Ingredients

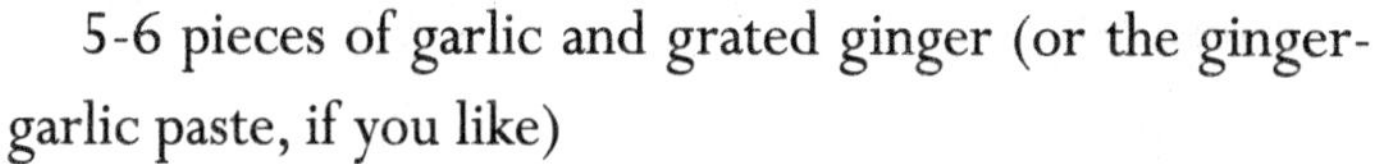

½ kg fish (Rohu or Surmai)

1 and ½ tsp methi

5-6 pieces of garlic and grated ginger (or the ginger-garlic paste, if you like)

2-3 tbsp of curd

1 tsp of turmeric and chilli powder

Salt to taste

Preparation

Pour oil in a kadhai and heat it. Add the methi. After it becomes brown, add the fish. Put in the curd, haldi, chilli and the ginger-garlic. Stir well. Add salt.

Then smash the fish well.

Then remove it from the stove and serve.

Fried aloo bhindi

Ingredients

1/4 kg of ladyfinger
2 large onions
4 tbsp oil
2 big potatoes
2 tbsp of besan
½ tbsp of coriander powder
¼ tbsp of amchoor powder
1 tsp of chilli powder
1 tsp of haldi
Salt to your taste

Preparation

Wash the ladyfinger and then cut them into small pieces in any shape of your choice. Make sure you dry them thoroughly after washing them.

Wash the potatoes and cut them into thin long pieces. Slice the onions.

Mix all the powders with the ladyfinger, potatoes and onions nicely.

Take a small kadhai. Put the oil in it and heat it well.

Add the ladyfinger, potatoes and onion mixture and fry well till it is deep brown.

Fried (Banarasi/south Indian potatoes)

Ingredients

½ kg potatoes
½ tbsp coriander
½ tbsp amchoor powder
1 tsp turmeric powder
1 tsp of chilli powder
1 tsp of ajwain
2 tbsp cooking oil
Salt to taste

Preparation

Boil the potatoes. Peel them and cut them into medium pieces and mix them with the amchoor powder, coriander powder, turmeric powder and chilli powder.

Now take a small kadhai, add oil and heat it well.

Add ajwain and when it is done, put the potatoes mixed with mixture in it and stir well.

After 5 minutes, turn off the flame and serve after letting it rest awhile.

Vegetable korma with coconut milk

Ingredients

½ kg beans
½ kg shelled peas
2 large pieces of carrot
2 potatoes
2 tomatoes
1 small cauliflower
¼ tbsp sambhar powder
1 tsp turmeric powder
1 green chilli
1 pod of garlic
1 small piece of ginger
1 tbsp coriander powder
1 tbsp poppy seeds
4-6 cloves
4-6 pieces of cinnamon
2-4 bay leaves
4 small cardamoms
2 cups of coconut milk
2 onions
2 tbsp oil

Lemon juice to taste
Salt to taste

Preparation

Cut all the vegetables.

Then take the masala powders, along with one cut onion, chopped garlic and grated ginger and put it in a grinder to make a paste.

Chop the remaining onions.

Take the oil and heat it in a vessel. Add the cardamoms, cloves, bay leaves and cinnamon, and after slight frying, add the onions and make them brown.

Put the masala paste in and fry it along with chopped tomatoes.

Put the vegetables in along with salt and stir it well.

After a while add 4 cups of water, let it boil and cook.

After the vegetables are cooked, put in the coconut milk and let it heat.

But see to it that you don't boil the milk.

Then, once it has settled and the dish is off the flame, add lemon juice and garnish with green coriander leaves.

Methi chicken

Ingredients

6 pieces of chicken
1 tbsp coriander powder
1 tsp chilli powder
1 tsp cinnamon and clove powder
1 large onion
100 gm fresh methi
1 tsp cumin seeds powder
2 tbsp of oil
Salt to taste

Preparation

Take a kadhai, put in chopped onions and fry them till they are brown.

Put in chicken along with all the spices. Fry it for a while.

Put some water and let it cook.

After the chicken is done and water is almost dry, put in the green methi and fry it well.

Galavat kabab (mutton/ chicken)

Ingredients

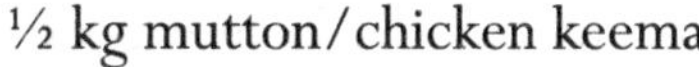

½ kg mutton/chicken keema
2 large onions
1 pod of garlic
1 medium-sized piece of ginger
One small piece of raw papaya (only if using mutton)
4 cloves
4 small pieces of cinnamon sticks
1 tbsp of curd
3 tbsp oil
2 chillies (you can avoid it, if you so wish to. One chilli would be desirable)
Fresh coriander leaves
Salt to taste

Preparation

Cut the onions into medium-sized pieces, then fry them deep brown.

Make a paste of garlic, ginger and onions; and make a powder of cinnamon, cloves and red chillies. (If it is mutton, add papaya with the paste.)

Mix the paste with the keema, salt, fresh coriander and the curd.

Marinate for one hour.

Take a non-stick frying pan, add oil and put it on the stove.

Make small round-shaped patties and shallow fry them in the oil till done. No deep frying.

Serve with raw onions (optional).

Very few things defeated Sumitra. One of them was the north Indian chapati. She always felt she could never tackle the breads—rotis, pooris and parathas. So that is the one thing she made sure I was adept at. Made to stand on high stools in the kitchen and roll out the dough and make rotis successfully was an art she made sure I mastered, precisely because she was just not interested in the obsession with the round and hot roti.

Sumitra | Sanskrit | सुमित्रा/ su:mitra: / *good friend* from the Sanskrit root 'su' meaning good, and 'mitra' meaning friend.

Anees | Arabic | أنيس | Arabic root, meaning friendly, friend, companion, close friend.

Afterword

by Vir Sanghvi

A few years ago, it was officially suggested that the most truly Indian dish was khichdi. Media stunts were staged where famous chefs made enormous quantities of khichdi for the cameras and we were told that this was the one dish that united India.

Well, yes and no. The dish that really unites India is dal, which you find nearly everywhere you go.

And on the subject of rice dishes, the one that unifies India is not khichdi. It is biryani (or pulao). People in the food business will tell you that everyone orders biryani. It is a celebratory dish, and it is a dish that feeds your sorrow—which may be why it was the most ordered take-away dish during the Covid-19 pandemic.

Even people who don't eat meat, order vegetarian biryani—which leads to arguments and fist fights: Can biryani be made without fish, meat or chicken?

There is a reason why khichdi gets official sanction and biryani does not.

In the current food mythology, biryani is treated as a dish brought here by Muslim invaders. Khichdi, on the other hand, was apparently invented by pious vegetarian Hindus who cooked it when the evil invaders left them alone.

Most of this, of course, is nonsense.

For a start, khichdi is not necessarily vegetarian. There are non-vegetarian khichdis all over India. The dish was even colonized during the Raj and it still turns up on country house breakfast tables in the UK, usually made with rice and smoked haddock and is called kedgeree, a corruption of the original word.

Nor is khichdi a symbol of the divide between the meat-crazy Muslim invaders and their grass-loving Hindu subjects. It was prepared regularly in the Mughal kitchen and there is a famous story about Emperor Akbar and his favourite courtier Birbal that revolves around khichdi. Akbar's son Jehangir was so fond of Gujarati khichdi that it gained in popularity during his reign and was regularly served in court. And the Emperor Aurangzeb, a hate figure in our times, served a version of khichdi in his court as well.

The characterization of biryani as an invading food is also bogus. The claim about its alleged foreign origin rests solely on the linguistic origin of the name.

The term 'biryani' is clearly derived from Persian and so, say some, it must have come from Persia. The problem with this theory is that Persian was the court language of the Mughals so linguistic origins can be misleading. There is certainly no rice dish in Iran called biryani or anything like it. (There is an Iranian dish with a similar name but it is not made with rice.)

We have records of biryani being cooked in the Mughal kitchen and very few references before that. So, was biryani invented in the kitchens of the Mughal court?

It is tempting to say yes, but the question does not yield an easy answer. There is, first of all, the problem of distinguishing between a biryani and a pulao.

The traditional answer is to say that in a biryani the rice and meat are cooked separately and then arranged in layers, before a final spell of cooking by steam.

Well, maybe.

But the most famous biryani in India, the classic biryani of Awadh, is called a pulao in Lucknow. I have spoken to many traditional chefs there who refuse to use the term biryani to describe their work. Some have even said contemptuously that a pulao only becomes a biryani when it is cooked in a huge handi for scores of people. The haute cuisine version can only be called a pulao.

Once you start using the terms pulao and biryani interchangeably, then the argument is transformed. A pulao can definitely be vegetarian. And its origins are even more complicated. There certainly are pulaos in the Middle East but there are also ancient Indian versions.

In the ancient Sangam literature there are references to various soru dishes (soru means rice) which correspond to what we call pulao today. Perun soru corresponds to what we would now call mutton pulao.

There are also linguistic clues. Words that sound like 'pulo' have long been used in Sanskrit literature to refer to meat and rice dishes similar to today's pulao. Food historian K.T. Achaya says, '...the word is ascribed to the Persian and Arabic pulao, yet it would appear to have found its way long ago into both Sanskrit and early Tamil Literature of the third and sixth centuries.' (This is before it turns up in Persian, Turkey or Arabic texts.)

So is biryani Persian or Indian? Is it different from pulao? Is pulao a Middle-Eastern dish? Or did it have an ancient south Indian counterpart?

I don't know what the answers to these questions are. I don't think anyone does. But they are worth asking because they capture the essential complexity of Indian food. Only a fool would say, confronted with all the evidence, that khichdi is Hindu while biryani came from Muslim invaders.

India is too complicated a country for such simplistic distinctions.

Then, let's take the confusion over kababs. We know that there have been kababs in Central Asia for generations. Most early cooks found it easy to cook meat or fowl on skewers over an open fire—which, in essence, is what a kabab is, whether you call it a shashlik or shish kabab.

But sometimes kababs turn up in forms that we don't easily identify as Islamic or Central Asian in origin, at first. Take the satay of Thai cuisine. It is almost certainly derived from the satay of Indonesia and Malaysia which, when you think about it, are no more than Far Eastern versions of kababs. They were introduced to the region by chefs from Western Asia, in imitation of the Middle East's kababs.

India's kababs, on the other hand, pose complex questions of religious identity. There is no doubt that Muslim traders, travellers and armies brought kababs with them.

But were kababs totally unfamiliar to Indians?

Consider the *Manasollasa*, a twelfth-century south Indian text. It includes recipes, among which is one for a meat dish in which the pieces are first marinated in fruit juice (to tenderize them) before being threaded on to skewers and then cooked on hot coals. This sounds a lot like later Middle-Eastern recipes for kababs.

As it seems unlikely that Persian and Arab chefs had access to the *Manasollasa*, the dishes were probably developed independently of each other. But was there a point, at some stage in our history, when the two traditions mingled and merged?

Or take the case of the tandoor which is where most restaurant-style Indian kababs are made these days. You find variations of the tandoor all over Central Asia. The names vary slightly, but it is clearly the same kind of oven.

So did the tandoor make its way to India from West and Central Asia? That would seem probable except that early prototypes of the tandoor have been discovered during excavations of Indus Valley sites. This, by itself, does not prove that the first tandoors originated in India. The people of the Indus Valley had strong trade links with civilizations such as Mesopotamia. The tandoor could have originated there and then come to India.

But what's important is this: We already had tandoors in the subcontinent long before, what we now call, Hinduism developed. And certainly, long before the Prophet was born.

So why make this a Hindu–Muslim argument? India predates both religions.

As interesting is the development of the tandoor in the twentieth century. Till the 1920s and '30s, the tandoor was used in north India just as it was in West and Central Asia: to make bread.

Then, sometime in the first half of the twentieth century, a restaurant in the city of Peshawar started putting marinated, skewered chickens into the tandoor. Thus, was born the first tandoori chicken.

Though Peshawar is now in Pakistan, at the time the town had Sikh, Hindu and Muslim inhabitants. The restaurant that invented tandoori chicken was owned by a man called Moka Singh. When he left the city after the Partition and ended up in Delhi, he let his former employees open a version of the restaurant in Old Delhi using the same name: Moti Mahal.

By the late 1950s, Moti Mahal had made tandoori chicken so famous that restaurants all over India began installing tandoors. Nobody had believed that a bread oven could be used so successfully to cook chicken till Moti Mahal showed how it could be done.

A whole family of dishes grew up around the tandoor: the chicken tikka (made with smaller pieces of the bird), the barrah kabab and eventually, butter chicken (made with the leftover bits of the tandoori chicken and the chicken tikka). Soon, even kababs that had once been cooked over an open flame or on charcoal began to be cooked in the tandoor. The seekh kabab, a dish that has a similar Iranian counterpart, and which had been cooked in India for decades, now began to be cooked in the tandoor.

Today, most kabab cooking in Indian restaurants is centred around the tandoor. Even Lucknow, home of such famous kababs as the galouti, which have always been made on a tawa, has adopted the tandoor and all kinds of tandoori kababs turn up on every menu. (Though, fortunately, the classic kababs are still cooked the old way!)

So, what are tandoori kababs? Hindu or Muslim? Indian or foreign? Indian food or invader food?

These are questions that hardly anyone in India ever bothered to ask. Restaurants that followed Moti Mahal's traditions and took them further upmarket, chose to name themselves after Central Asian cities where tandoori chicken was unknown: Bukhara, Samarkand, Kandahar. The waiters were usually dressed as Pathans and the suggestion was that this was food that came from the Afghan border or perhaps even further north. At a subconscious level, a Muslim origin was implied. Bukhara, Samarkand and Kandahar are hardly centres of ancient Hindu cuisine!

Nobody drew too much attention to the fact that many of the dishes had been invented by Punjabi Hindus in Daryaganj. (Except for the original tandoori chicken, all the later variations from chicken tikka to butter chicken were created in post-Partition Delhi.)

To me, the complexity of the kabab's origins—part Persian, part Central Asian, part Punjabi–Hindu, part ancient Indian—has always re-emphasized the glory of Indian cooking. It doesn't matter where anything (or anyone) originally came from. Once it (or they) got to India, everything was our own.

But not all of the complexity of Indian food is about Hindus and Muslims. One way of discovering this is a visit to the old city of Hyderabad.

I went there two years ago, determined to check out as many biryani places as I could. Hyderabadi biryani is a classic that developed over time. It emerged from the Mughal biryani tradition of Delhi. The story goes that when the Mughal emperors sent governors to the southern part of their empire (the Nizam-ul-Mulk, the predecessor of the Nizam of Hyderabad), they sent them on their way with full retinues of retainers and cooks.

The cooks came to love the spicy and sour flavour of the Deccan and adapted their biryanis to incorporate those new ingredients. They also prided themselves on making kacha biryanis, that is, biryanis in which the rice and meat were not cooked separately but where raw meat was cooked with the rice.

I have always found it hard to get good traditional biryanis in Hyderabad outside of private homes or from family caterers, so I wandered through the old city, trying all the famous places that I had heard of.

Frankly, none of the biryanis were very good though some were okay. But what intrigued me was that, even though the restaurants were full, and guests were lining up for tables, most people were not there for the biryani.

I should have guessed as much from the hoardings outside the restaurants. None of them bragged about the biryanis. Most advertised a completely different dish: gobi manchurian. And sometimes: chicken manchurian.

At Shadab, a famous Hyderabad restaurant, I scoured the menu in vain looking for the Hyderabad curries that foodies so admired. Instead, the section of the menu that was called 'Curries (Non-Veg)' included 'Schezwan Chicken', 'Singapuri Chicken' and 'Lemon Chicken'. (They also had tandoori mutton masala, chicken tikka masala and butter chicken—all tributes to the influence of Moti Mahal.) All around me, diners were wolfing down mixed noodles and dishes with thick, cornflour-filled, red, 'Chinese' gravies.

I shouldn't have been surprised. It is pretty much the same story in nearly every Indian city or town. The last time I went to the Daryaganj Moti Mahal I was intrigued to see that it now had a 'Chinese' section on its menu. It didn't matter if the restaurant was run by Hindus or Muslims. They made their money serving 'Chinese' food.

Indian-Chinese food took just thirty years to become a country-wide craze. And today, I reckon it is second only to biryani in its popularity. Most intriguing: it is a cuisine that no Chinese person will be familiar with.

Till 1974, most Chinese restaurants in India were run by members of India's Chinese community. The Indian-Chinese were usually Hakkas whose ancestors had first come to Calcutta at the turn of the twentieth century.

The Indian-Chinese did not serve the food they ate at home at their restaurants. Instead, they served a largely inauthentic menu of global Chinese food that had been popularized by Chinese restaurants in America. Their restaurants did well. But not well enough for non-Chinese restaurateurs to take much interest in the sector.

That changed in 1974 when the Taj Mahal Hotel opened its Golden Dragon in Mumbai, serving the spicy food of the Sichuan region, which was nothing like the Chinese food Indians were used to. In 1978, the Taj group opened The House of Ming at its Delhi hotel, serving roughly the same menu as Mumbai's Golden Dragon.

At first the Indian Chinese restaurateurs were flabbergasted. Most of them had never been further east than Chowringhee. They had no idea what Sichuan food was. But the smarter ones quickly realized that the jig was up. Now that Indians had discovered that Chinese food could be hot and spicy, nobody was going to order American Chop Suey.

The restaurateurs decided not to copy the authentic Sichuan menus—that was beyond their core competence and besides, they did not have access to the Sichuan ingredients the Taj imported. So they evolved their own spicy dishes, often relying on such Indian flavour combinations as ginger-garlic paste and green chillies. They added lots of soya sauce to everything and when that was not enough, tomato ketchup.

By the 1990s, Indian-Chinese food was everywhere. And in the twenty-first century, vegetarian versions of the cuisine were invented while such archetypal dishes as chicken manchurian began to be recognized as junk-food classics in their own right.

All that explained the signs for gobi manchurian and the rush for Indian-Chinese dishes in the old city of Hyderabad. As far as the diners were concerned, Indian-Chinese was just another regional cuisine like, say, tandoori cooking.

How Indian would Indian-Chinese cuisine seem to today's politicians with their desire to go back to the food of an imaginary past where everyone was vegetarian and no foreign influences invaded our purely Hindu culture?

In reality, the imaginary pure-veg, pure-Hindu past never existed. Archaeologists have found evidence of cow-eating in excavations of Indus Valley sites, and during such much-lauded (by Hindu nationalists) eras as the Mauryan Empire, the people ate reptiles and frogs.[6]

The campaign to deny India its gastronomic heritage ignores the fact that for Indians, culinary invention and exchange have always been continuous and rewarding processes.

The Europeans gave us the chilli, the potato and tomato (all New World vegetables) and we turned them into staples of our cuisine.

How many Indians recognize that tea is not Indian? It is Chinese, and the first gardens in India were planted by the British. The Brits needed a cheap source of tea to service their domestic market so that they could undercut Chinese tea merchants. Tea-drinking did not really take off in India till the 1950s. Nor is coffee Indian. It is Arab. An enterprising Indian stole the beans from Arabia and planted them in south India.

With almost everything that we have taken from the rest of the world, we have made improvements and introduced refinements.

Much of the Western world now thinks of the samosa as Indian. In fact, it is a Middle-Eastern turnover, versions of which can still be found in several West Asian countries. But because the Indian version of the dish is the most accessible, it is the one that has enjoyed the greatest global success. So it is with the jalebi, another Middle-Eastern dish we have transformed to create the finest version.

The campaign to look inward to some mythical past leads us to ignore the triumphs of India's culinary engagement with the rest of the world. All food historians will tell you that the Arabs took rice to Europe. The paella of Spain and the risotto of Italy both have their origins in the rice that Arabs taught Europeans to eat.

But here's the key question: West Asia is not the ideal fertile ground for rice, which is not even native to the region. So who introduced the Arabs to rice?

There are two possible answers. But they both amount to the same thing: Indians.

We know that when Alexander of Macedon's army arrived in India in 326 BCE, its soldiers had never ever heard of rice. They were so astonished by it that they took rice back with them on the long painful journey to Europe and, it is speculated, introduced it to the Middle East on the way home. (Alexander died in Babylon in 323 BCE on that journey.)

A second theory is that when the Arabs conquered Sind in 711 CE, they discovered rice. (If that's true then it makes you wonder if the pulao traffic was one way.)

And as for tandoori chicken, here's one more fact to puzzle over. We recognize that early tandoors were found in Indus Valley sites. But do we also realize that the chicken was first domesticated by the Indus Valley Civilization? Our ancestors took a wild bird, bred it and put it on the world's dining tables.

That is the glory of Indian civilization, of how we have given so much to the world and how we have absorbed everything the world has given to us. It doesn't matter if it was once Hindu or once Muslim. Whether it came from Persia or, even, from China. Once it got here, we made it Indian.

These are historical facts that are hard to refute. So politicians bury them and tell lies instead. Biryani is not Indian, they say. Only khichdi is fully Hindu and truly Indian. Kababs must be Muslim because they are non-vegetarian.

Food is not the only area where such lies are spread. In fact, the lies about food are part of a larger drive to invent a bogus past for India. History books must be rewritten because the truth does not conform to political fantasy.

There are precedents for this. The Nazis did something similar by creating a bogus history where a race of Aryan supermen ruled. (Though admittedly the Nazis were more interested in controlling what came out of people's mouths, their successors are as interested in restricting what goes into our mouths.)

The deceit starts early: these lies are taught to schoolchildren who are too young to know better so the untruths acquire a certain menacing power. And a hate-filled future is sought to be built on an imaginary past.

Fortunately, food relies not just on knowledge but on the senses. All the brainwashing does not reach the palate. And as we have seen over the last few years, our senses are not so easy to fool.

Say what you will about Hindus and Muslims, dismiss good food as the cuisine of invaders and India will pay no attention. Biryani will still be the country's most ordered dish. Samosas will remain our favourite teatime snack. And at every Hindu wedding, the longest queue at the dinner buffet will be for jalebis.

Because food has no religion. And it is the truest expression of the unifying, pluralistic spirit of India.

Notes

1. 19 February 2017, PM campaigning in Uttar Pradesh. https://www.hindustantimes.com/assembly-elections/if-a-kabristan-can-be-constructed-so-should-a-shamshaan-pm-modi/story-obPfbdpUwPZm98wBKdZmTN.html
2. The Supreme Court judgment: https://www.sci.gov.in/pdf/JUD_2.pdf
3. The Supreme Court judgment: https://main.sci.gov.in/supremecourt/2017/19702/19702_2017_Judgement_08-Mar-2018.pdf
4. https://main.sci.gov.in/supremecourt/2017/19702/19702_2017_Judgement_08-Mar-2018.pdf
5. Charu Gupta, 'Hindu Women, Muslim Men: Love Jihad and Conversions', *Economic and Political Weekly*, Vol. 44, Issue No. 51, 19 December 2009.

6. D.N. Jha, *The Myth of the Holy Cow*, Navayana Publishing, 2009; first published by Matrix Books, 2001. Colleen Taylor Sen, *Feasts and Fasts: A History of Food in India*, Reaktion Books, 2014. Suryanarayan et. al., 'Lipid residues in pottery from the Indus Civilisation in northwest India', *Journal of Archaelogical Science*, Vol. 125, January 2021.

Appendix

In the process of sorting out my late father's things, amongst some carefully saved papers, I found a large yellow office file with just two letters punched in place.

One letter was written by Anees' father, Syed Mohd Chishti, from Deoria to his Hindu daughter-in-law, Sumitra, welcoming her into the fold.

The other was written by Sumitra's elder brother, D. Shankar Singh, from his home in Mysore, to Anees, his new brother-in-law. Shankar Singh was Sumitra's guardian after their parents' untimely death.

Neither S.M. Chishti nor D. Shankar Singh were able to attend the wedding, but they were the most important pillars of strength that enabled the young couple to soon find acceptance in each other's homes.

There is also an inscription in Jean Paul Sartre's *The Words* that I stumbled upon. It is from Anees to Sumitra, scribbled a year before they got married.

Letter from Syed Mohd Chishti in Deoria to Sumitra, dated 6 February 1966.

S. M. Chishti
Advocate
DEORIA

Date 6.2.66 196

My dear daughter,

I received your letter sometime back. I regret I could not reply earlier.

It is gratifying to know that you are now comfortably settled in your new house. Refrigerator was a necessity to you & it is good that you now possess one.

I am glad to learn that you two are leading a happy & joyful life. May God grant both of you a happy & prosperous future. Anees has told us all about you. I hope you will continue

I am progressing gradually but the disease which has afflicted me is of such a nature that in future I will have to lead a limited life. It will still take several weeks before I resume my routine work.

We have received the photographs sent by Shrees. I suppose you must have received letter from your mother-in-law.

With best wishes
Yours
S.K. [illegible]

Letter from D. Shankar Singh in Mysore to Anees, dated 29 January 1966.

Mysore 5
Date 29.1.66

My dear Mr. Anees

Thank you very much for your kind letter and glad to note the contents. First I want to congratulate you on marrying Sumitra. only thing I felt I would have been so much pleased to have been there in Dehali at the time of your marriage. Does not matter It is all God's will & human being is not the deciding factor.

I well come both of you to Mysore and spend atleast fifteen days with us. Please make the programme in that manner. Always Sumitra wants to run to Dehali. But Now. if she comes with you, It may not be the case

as it was before.

As you are an well educated &

cultured man I need not advise you

anything. (As you say we are the ~~~~

sons of this ~~sacred soil~~)

My blessings and good wishes for

your happy married life.

Yours most affly

D. Shankar Singh

My ~~dear Sumitra~~ As I have written to your

husband I need not write any thing to you

separately. I will [illegible] of you to

Mysore. Please write well in advance

with best wishes

Your loving brother

D. Shankar Singh

Inscription on a copy of *The Words* by Jean Paul Sartre: Anees for Sumitra.

For Sumitra,
who inspired me,
with her versatile leaps into various fields
of creativity —
— Absurd, Sartre, Camus;
Von Gogh, Sher-Gil;
Beckett, Brecht;
Tinbergen, and also Chaplin;

— and for my sake —

Agreed to tend towards
new, though dry, areas —
— Statistics, Quantum Physics,
Naipaul,
and, yes, even Cricket.

— Anees
14.1.65

Anees
Dec, '65

Index

Recipe Index

Acknowledgements

Prof. Shahid Amin is such a fine historian, but is mostly an indulgent bhaijan to me and such an inspiration. My gratitude to him for writing about his mamun despite pressing work engagements.

My late aunt Pratima Devi, my mother's sister-in-law, helped fill in many blanks in Sumitra's story. I am grateful to her and my cousins S. Vijayalakshmi, S.V. Rajendra Singh 'Babu' and Jairaj Singh, who reminded me of so much that was worth treasuring about my mother.

Thanks to Vir Sanghvi, gracious and willing to share in this enterprise with his thoughts on syncretic Indian food.

Thank you, Kaushik Dasgupta.

My publishers deserve my thanks, especially Siddhesh Inamdar, for his patience, and Tanima Saha. The book would not have been possible but for Krishan Chopra, who first thought the idea was publishable and pushed me to stay the course. Simar Puneet, my editor, helped shape, question and improve the narrative to make it much more meaningful. Jerry Singh, thanks for connecting us.

Abdul Jabbar and Hari Bahadur are also inheritors of my mother's recipes and have kept them alive over the years, well after her departure. Hari especially has helped me fill in some important blanks. Thank you, Upinder for typing up Sumitra's handwritten recipe book.

Thanks to my friends, family, colleagues and comrades—all of whom through conversations, debates and arguments allowed several ideas to take shape. Most of all, thanks to India, in general, for enabling Sumitra and Anees to be themselves and live a shared life.

About the Author

Seema Chishti has grown up, studied, lived and worked in Delhi as a journalist-writer for three decades. Her family ties to Uttar Pradesh, Karnataka and Andhra Pradesh have meant a long engagement with these states over the years. She is interested in politics, society, questions of identity and technology, and in examining the changes in information and digital space and their impact on our democracy and on the way we live. She is the co-author of *Note by Note*: *The India Story (1947-2017)* and has worked with the BBC in London and India, *The Indian Express* and HTV.

About the Author

[illegible]